REDEMPTION

GOD'S POWER TO REACH THE LEAST, THE LAST, AND THE LOST

True Stories of God's Redeeming Mercy

DOUGLAS F. WALL

FOREWORD BY DR. KEN BLUE

REDEMPTION
God's Power to Reach the Least, the Last and the Lost

Printed in the USA
ISBN: 978-1-939944-18-4

Library of Congress Control Number: 2013953728

Cover Design & Interior Formatting: Wendy K. Walters

Published By KINGDOM HOUSE PUBLISHING | Lakebay, Washington, USA

To Contact the author:

www.pureforge.com
email: dwall@pureforge.com
office: 760.201.0955
mobile: 858.243.3777

To Jesus, my redeemer.

REDEMPTION (THEOLOGY)
AS DEFINED BY WIKIPEDIA*

As a theological concept redemption is an element of salvation that broadly means the deliverance from sin. Leon Morris says that "Paul uses the concept of redemption primarily to speak of the saving significance of the death of Christ." The English word redemption means 'repurchase' or 'buy back', and in the Old Testament referred to the ransom of slaves (Exodus 21:8). In the New Testament the redemption word group is used to refer both to deliverance from sin and freedom from captivity. Theologically, redemption is a metaphor for what is achieved through the Atonement. Therefore, there is a metaphorical sense in which the death of Jesus pays the price of a ransom, releasing Christians from bondage to sin and death.

ACKNOWLEDGEMENTS

I would like to give thanks and acknowledgements
to all those who have inspired me to write this book,
including all of my family members, friends,
mentors and advisors, especially my wife, children,
and grandchild. I am extremely grateful to so many . . .
you know who you are.
Thank you.

REDEMPTION

WHAT OTHERS ARE SAYING

Doug is the most positive "make things happen" guy I know. Nothing dampens his enthusiasm for what God does in the world, in business, and in relationships. He is a master story-teller of it all, to boot!

DR. RON JENSON

Co-Founder and Chairman, Future Achievement, Higher Ground,
Kingdom Marketplace Partners
San Diego, CA

The passion and energy of the author is reflected in each and every short story. Difficult to put the book down. This is a must read for everyone!

N.K. MECKEL

A Discoverer of God's Inventions
President, C.T.O., Co-Founder of PureForge®
San Diego, CA

If dealing with the hardships of life has always baffled you, this book will provide you comfort in knowing you are not alone. Doug's story of stamina and discovery of God is powerful. You will not be able to stop turning the pages.

JACQUELINE TOWNSEND KONSTANTUROS

Chief Strategy Officer, The Townsend Team
San Diego, CA

This book is the story of how one man's life has been redeemed, but more broadly, of how God can redeem any and every man's life if given the opportunity to do so. Doug Wall is part of the new breed of corporate leaders who engage with their heart and spirit as well as their head in their work and calling—a highly relational leader who is not only oriented toward and motivated by quality and excellence and service, but also understands the dynamics and intracacies of leading people and building systems and processes and supply chains and value propositions and sustainable margins and business models in a global economy. Doug realizes and practices the importance and necessity of marrying and managing the corporate mission within the context of the broader societal mission and higher heavenly mission.

DR. BRUCE COOK

President and Founder, Kingdom House Publishing, KEYS Network,
VentureAdvisers.com, Inc.
Lakebay, WA

I have found Doug Wall to be an authentic leader in many areas: business, spiritual and family. Doug has a great passion for the lost and broken, and is a champion of underdogs and the poor. The heart of Jesus flows through his life. Excellence surrounds everything he touches and I was weeping at the powerful impact of this story. His transparency will touch your heart and as he shares, the revelation and experience will captivate you. It is filled with real life—where you cannot play hide and seek with God. It reveals God's heart towards all men to redeem what was lost and stolen. This book is filled with biblical truths and you will be drawn to finish it because of the emotional content. I could not put this book down!

DONALD LISLE

Founder & President, Lisle Insurance & Financial Services
Fresno, CA

What a friend we have in Jesus,
All our sins and griefs to bear!
What a privilege to carry
Everything to God in prayer!
Oh, what peace we often forfeit,
Oh, what needless pain we bear,
All because we do not carry
Everything to God in prayer!

Have we trials and temptations?
Is there trouble anywhere?
We should never be discouraged—
Take it to the Lord in prayer.
Can we find a friend so faithful,
Who will all our sorrows share?
Jesus knows our every weakness;
Take it to the Lord in prayer.

Are we weak and heavy-laden,
Cumbered with a load of care?
Precious Savior, still our refuge—
Take it to the Lord in prayer.
Do thy friends despise, forsake thee?
Take it to the Lord in prayer!
In His arms He'll take and shield thee,
Thou wilt find a solace there.

Blessed Savior, Thou hast promised
Thou wilt all our burdens bear;
May we ever, Lord, be bringing
All to Thee in earnest prayer.
Soon in glory bright, unclouded,
There will be no need for prayer—
Rapture, praise, and endless worship
Will be our sweet portion there.

—Joseph M. Scriven 1855

I CALL YOUR NAME

Jesus I call Your name
Will you heal my darkest pain?

I've been afraid to laugh or cry
I know you loved me enough to die

But this pain is dark and deep
How I long for You to keep

Jesus show me the darkness in my heart
That won't allow this pain to part

Jesus I know you're inside of me
And only you can set me free

You are my shepherd I am a lamb
And you love me for who I am

Jesus I call Your name
Thank you for taking my darkest pain

Douglas F. Wall

EVERY DAY IS A NEW DAY OF REDEMPTION!

TABLE OF CONTENTS

FOREWORD

Without formal theological training, Doug Wall is, nevertheless, a theologian. He knows the Bible, knows God personally and sees the ups and downs of life with the love and redeeming providence of God in the middle of it all. In this book, Doug discloses God's activity in his own life, which, in turn, helps readers see God's activity in theirs. That makes him a pastoral theologian.

A theologian at heart, Doug has been my friend for nearly 23 years and I can assure you that what he says in this book about God's redemptive love is genuine. True, he is inherently optimistic and resilient – a gift that came to him in his genetic code – but he has also chosen to see life as an adventure guided by God's providence.

Over the years, he has succeeded in business and become one of the best connected businessmen in Southern California. No problem with celebrating God's redemptive care in all of this. But, what about the death of two children? How does one recover from this, let alone see God's redemption in it? Somehow, Doug is able to. Is he naïve or does he actually know the heart of the Father? Read and see for yourself. We often hear that it's not what happens to us, but how we respond to our ups and downs that makes or breaks us.

The secret of Doug's hopefulness and playful sense of adventure is that he sees God working through everything from the death of a child to business success. His firm belief in redemption gets him up when he is knocked down and shows him who to thank when all is going well. The personal stories are not only uplifting, but also exhortations to actually trust in the Father's providential care. In reading them, we can all learn and grow.

— Ken Blue

Pastor, Motivational Speaker, Best-Selling Author

PREFACE

I am a passionate man. Everyone who knows me well will attest to that fact. I am passionate about my wife, children, grandchild, friends, partners, co-workers, and life! I am most passionate about Jesus, my savior and my redeemer!

My life is one continuous adventure whether I'm on a mission trip to Romania or establishing a start-up company in Southern California. There is never a dull moment and every day I'm eager to see what God has in store for me. I rejoice in each day! I've learned that the Holy Spirit dwells in me and helps me with every detail of my life. Everything matters and has meaning, even the ordinary and mundane, including how I treat people, how I react to stressful situations, and how much I trust God. And, in His unlimited and unending love, He redeems all of my wounds, transgressions, and failures.

Redemption is not just the restoration process but it is also the complete deliverance and freedom from the bondage of sin.

All through my life, the Lord has redeemed it all. His grace is overwhelming. This book shares some of my personal stories of God's redeeming mercy.

"He has sent redemption to His people; He has commanded His covenant forever; holy and awesome is His name."

Psalm 111:9 (NKJV)

"In Him we have redemption through His blood, the forgiveness of sins, according to the riches of His grace which He caused to abound toward us in all wisdom and prudence."

Ephesians 1:7-8 (NKJV)

CHAPTER 1

JUST TWO
HOURS AWAY

W hat a wonderful surprise it was when, during my wife's
Cesarean section, the doctors delivered two beautiful girls:
surprise, fraternal twins! We named our daughters Jessica and
Courtney, and fell immediately in love with their delicate features,
cute little noses, and big beautiful eyes. Jessica's name means
"He sees," (God watches over us) and Courtney's name means "of
the court" (God gives us nobility). They were born on my mom's
birthday, July 22, 1988.

THREE MONTHS LATER

It was a beautiful Sunday morning, October 30, 1988. Time seems to slow down on the days that change is about to occur. My wife, Therese, and I had just left our hotel in Palm Springs to go to church before coming back home in a suburb of San Diego. I had convinced Therese that we needed to get away for the weekend. We had three girls all in diapers and it was going to be a nice little getaway. Our first born, Melissa, was two, and Courtney and Jessie (Jessica) were only three months old. We were going to be just two hours away. If anything went wrong, we could be home in two hours.

We decided to call home to see how our girls were doing. We just wanted to make sure everything was okay.

I still remember the size and weight of the cell phone that was built into our white Jeep Cherokee. I was expecting my mom to answer since she had come over to stay at our house to watch our little girls. What was very unusual was to hear my dad's voice on the phone since he would typically stay at their own home when my mom came over to watch the girls for us. I remember the sinking feeling I had when I heard my dad's voice because I could immediately tell he was crying and that something was terribly wrong. I was 31 years old and at that time I only remembered my dad crying once before. That day was the day he found out that his father had died. My dad grew up during the Depression and his family and friends were very unemotional and pragmatic. He was just not the type of person who showed very much emotion.

My dad was so upset he could only say to me "get home quick ... something has happened" and then he suddenly hung up. The silence on the other end of the phone left me hanging. I immediately thought the worst had happened. I imagined that my mom and our three little girls had been killed in a car crash. My mind actually went numb and I went into a state of shock. I could not hide the fear and terror in my eyes. Therese kept asking me in a panic, "What's wrong? What's wrong?" But, I couldn't answer. She knew that something terrible had happened. We immediately turned the car toward home and continued to try calling back to find out what had happened. The phone just kept ringing. No answer. Finally, after several tries, my dad answered the phone and told us that Courtney (our second twin) had died suddenly in the middle of the night of crib death—SIDS (Sudden Infant Death Syndrome).

Time suddenly stopped for what seemed an eternity right then. That moment is forever frozen in my mind. The power of those chilling words, "Courtney died," was overwhelming and is still overwhelming as I write this decades later. My mind and body went into deep shock and I had to pull the car over and weep. I had such a hard time telling Therese that our daughter had died. I could not find any words to say. I tried to talk but nothing came out . . . I finally blubbered it out and we wept on the side of the freeway like we have never cried before or since.

> My mind and body went into deep shock and I had to pull the car over and weep.

I could still see Courtney and Jessica in the little bassinettes when we said goodbye just two days before. I was having a hard time believing that this horrible thing had just happened. This was by far the most difficult and absolute lowest and darkest time of my life.

The next two weeks are a blur to me; the drive home, meeting with family members, the days leading up to the funeral and the miserable days after the funeral. By the time we got home, Courtney's body had already been taken to the funeral home. Therese was compelled to go to the funeral home to find closure. I did not accompany her, but her sister, brother and family did. As Therese entered the funeral home, the Holy Spirit told her, "Courtney is not here; she's with Me," and the peace of God fell on her. From that point on, Therese's healing began.

Therese asked me to go with her that day to the funeral home but I could not bear to go and see my daughter's lifeless face and body. It was just too much . . . too overwhelming. I just did not have the courage to go face to face with the death of my own child. I was afraid to look into lifeless eyes, especially knowing that this used to be my child. I know I missed out on God's gift of peace that day. Instead, I began to shut down all of my feelings and just went through the motions. I did not cry at the funeral. I pretended to be strong and tried to appear that I was holding it all together.

The reality is that my confidence and my faith were completely shattered. This time of my life is by far the darkest, lowest, and loneliest point. Parents don't expect to outlive their children. I know I certainly did not. Before Courtney died, I had visions and dreams of our beautiful twin girls growing up . . . I could see them as teenagers full of joy and laughing. By far, her death was one of the most difficult things to deal with . . . the deep sense of loss for a life lost before its time. Additionally, I could not shake the feelings of shame because I was not there when it happened. I told myself that I should not have talked my wife into leaving that weekend. I truly believed that Courtney's death was my fault and I was going to have to live with this guilt the rest of my life. I was now imprisoned within walls of hopelessness and despair.

The book of Job reveals Job's despair as well as the redemptive power of God's word: *"Naked I came from my mother's womb, and naked I will depart. The LORD gave and the LORD has taken away; . . . I loathe my very life; therefore I will give free rein to my complaint and speak out in the bitterness of my soul . . . I know that You can do all things; no plan of Yours can be thwarted. You asked, 'Who is this that obscures my counsel without knowledge?' Surely I spoke of things I did not understand, things too wonderful for me to know"* (Job 1:21, 10:1, 42:2-3 NKJV).

"Blessed are those who mourn,
for they shall be comforted."

Matthew 5:4 (NKJV)

"Get busy living, or get busy dying!"

Red: *Shawshank Redemption*

The Lord redeems the death
of each and every child.

Douglas F. Wall

REDEMPTION

CHAPTER 2

GIVE SCOTTY TO ME!

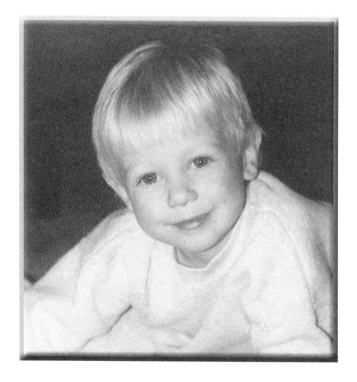

After Courtney died, the doctors, counselors, and Sudden Infant Death Syndrome (SIDS) experts told us there was a very high risk that Jessica, our surviving twin daughter, could also die from SIDS. They also told us to wait for six months before we started trying to have another child.

Additionally, the professionals recommended that we connect Jessica to an infant sleep apnea monitor, which is an electrical device that monitors the breathing of the baby to make sure that the breaths are not spaced too far apart. I remember that we set the monitor for 20 seconds, which would mean that if her breaths were spaced more than 20 seconds apart, the monitor would sound an alarm and hopefully wake us up in time so we could provide emergency resuscitation procedures until the paramedics arrived. Therese and I learned how to perform CPR for infants just in case of an emergency. This particular baby monitor incorporated wires and electrodes that were placed on Jessie's tiny little chest. I remember clearly that our little Jessie did not particularly like the tangle or the feel of all of these annoying wires and probes. Not only were they cold to her skin but they were intrusive. Jessie was constantly kicking and pulling the monitors off in the middle of the night.

Between the long, separated breaths and Jessie pulling off the lead wires, we must have averaged one false alarm every night for six or seven months. Sometimes the monitor would go off three or four times in the same night, which created a very stressful living environment for our family. Therese and I became light sleepers because we were always in a heightened state of panic thinking that this could be the night our little Jessie stops breathing. Neither one of us got a good night's sleep during Jessie's infancy. Our two children were being raised in an atmosphere of anxiety and panic.

Shortly after Courtney's death, Therese became pregnant again. Our first three children were girls so we were expecting another girl. The two previous births were Cesarean (C-Section) deliveries. The doctors scheduled our third C-Section on September 5, 1989. As the doctors pulled the baby out of the womb, they told us, "It's a boy!" We were just not expecting a boy. I could not believe I actually had a son! My first son! I was completely overjoyed. We were going to name him Daniel, but he just didn't look like a Daniel. He looked like

Scott. We loved the name Scott and we immediately and lovingly started calling him Scotty. When I was growing up, there was a song on the radio by Bobby Goldsboro called "Watching Scotty Grow." For some reason, I always connected with that song as a child, as if God was preparing me for my own son and fatherhood.

When Scotty was approximately 18 months old, he had a very high fever and Therese and I were very worried about him. When you've lost a child, any illness with your other children is cause for alarm. We were debating whether we should take him to the hospital, but I decided to pray for him first.

I began reading in Genesis 22 where the Lord spoke to Abraham and said: *"Take now your son, your only son, Isaac, whom you love. And go into the land of Moriah, and offer him there for a burnt offering upon one of the mountains which I will name you."* I was sitting on the couch with Scotty cradled in my left arm with my right hand on his forehead feeling his temperature. As I prayed for him, the Lord spoke to me through this scripture, and I felt as if He was saying to me, "Give Scotty to Me." I paused and thought about what the Lord was asking, and I just flatly said back to Him, "No, I can't do it!" I just could not understand why God would ask a father to sacrifice his only son.

A few moments later, as I continued praying, the Lord spoke to me again, and said, "Give Scotty to Me."

Looking back on this moment, I am still in wonder and in awe that God had so much patience and allowed me to vent my anger and frustration with him and tell him how I really felt! I told the Creator of the universe who has all power and wisdom that I just cannot obey him. It's too much to ask me to sacrifice my only son and I just didn't have that much faith. I reasoned with God and flatly and firmly told Him that He had enough babies in heaven and I just couldn't let Him take my Scotty. Lastly, I reasoned with the Lord that one baby funeral is enough for any father to handle in life. I was dead serious!

> My conflict was real. I was afraid of death. Should I trust God?

A few moments went by and the Lord, very patiently and lovingly, spoke to me a third time with even more love, patience and gentleness: "Give Scotty to Me." Weeping, I closed my eyes and I could see His arms stretched out to me. My conflict was real. I was afraid of death. Should I trust God?

Very slowly and reluctantly, I closed my eyes and pictured myself giving Scotty to the Lord. I could see Scotty's blue eyes looking up at me, and I could actually visualize placing my son in Jesus' open arms . . . and Jesus taking him from me.

At that very moment, I felt Scotty's fever leave.

Then, I sensed the Lord's smile and He gave Scotty right back to me. As I wept, I could feel God's mercy assuring me that my heavenly Father trusts me to be Scotty's father. Suddenly, the burden that I was carrying of guilt, shame, and disappointment for not being a better father was lifted off of me and I could feel the weight of all my failures actually leave my body. The Lord truly does redeem us and sets us free from our disappointments, our shame, even our guilty conscience, and truly does fill us with hope.

"By faith Abraham, being tested, offered up Isaac, And he who had received the promises offered up his only-begotten son, of whom it was said that in Isaac your Seed shall be called, concluding that God was able to raise him up, even from the dead, from where he even received him, in a figure."

Hebrews 11: 17-19 (NKJV)

The Lord redeems our children and sets us free from disappointment, shame and guilt.

Douglas F. Wall

REDEMPTION

CHAPTER 3

REDEMPTION IN UTAH

Januray 6, 1991, our family began attending Foothills Church pastored by Ken Blue. Ken had written a book titled *Authority to Heal*, and was considered by many leaders to be an authority on praying for the sick. Therese and I knew at once in our spirits that this was going to be our new church home. We made friends immediately and loved Ken's matter-of-fact, no-nonsense approach to teaching and discipleship, as well as his keen insights on the spiritual world.

Just a week after finding our new church, I had a dream that woke me in the middle of the night. The dream was very vivid and frightening, and I remember the details even to this day.

I was in a large business conference meeting and I decided to get up and go to meet people in one of the back rooms. There, I found several businessmen, dressed in suits, preparing bodies for burial in coffins. There was a pentagram sign hanging on the wall. I looked around the room and noticed an entrance to a stairwell made of ancient dark gray stone, which appeared to be leading down to a castle dungeon. I remember thinking to myself, "How interesting it would be to go down into this dungeon to meet Satan and to see what hell is like." Curiosity took over and as I started to enter through this gateway and descend the stone stairway, a businessman wearing an evil mask was coming up the stairs toward me. As he passed me, I calmly asked him, "Is this some kind of game?" The businessman replied back to me in a matter of fact manner, "No, this is business!"

I distinctly remember as I started to walk down the winding stairway that my senses were much more heightened. I noticed the moss growing between the cracks, the feel of the stone under my feet, the musty smell and flickering light of the oil torches. As I continued to descend, I noticed the temperature was getting colder and colder and the light from the torches was getting dimmer and dimmer. I also noticed that the shadows were lengthening. Up to this point, I thought this was only a dream and I could always wake up and it would be over. But suddenly, I no longer had control of my legs; I was being swept into this pit of darkness by a force pulling me down. I was now traveling faster and faster and for the first time I was aware that this was not a dream, and I was getting a firsthand look at hell.

A fear came over me that was more intense than any fear I had ever experienced. I cried out to God and I felt like I was in a tug of war, with darkness pulling me down to hell and light pulling me up. I was in the middle of a terrifying and horrifying battle. I finally cried out to Jesus! Suddenly, I regained control of my legs and started running up the stairs, fleeing for my life, trying to get away from this ghostlike, smoke spirit that was chasing me.

I ran up and up, until I was finally at the top of a tall tower full of light and the smoke spirit was no longer chasing me. As I looked out from the top of this tower, I could now see a huge empty stadium.

Waking up, I was still shaking with fright and gasping as if I had just run a sprint. I woke up my wife and told her the dream; we prayed, and I finally went back to sleep.

A few weeks later, I went on a skiing trip to Brian Head, Utah, with five other business friends and acquaintances. The trip was to be a fun-filled, relaxing time, but after the first day of skiing, things took a bizarre turn. I noticed a pornographic magazine lying on the kitchen counter. I looked away immediately because pornography was something I had battled in my youth. I thought turning away would be enough, but later that evening, as we played poker, I began breaking out in hives on my face, neck, hands, arms, legs, and even inside my mouth. My friends asked if I was okay.

I said no, and excused myself from the poker game and went to lie down. As I lay there on my bed, I started feeling much worse. My stomach felt like someone had stuck a knife deep into my belly. I heard the voice of the Lord say, "Have Jerry pray for you." I was embarrassed to ask Jerry to pray for me because I wasn't sure if he even believed in prayer. As the pain in my belly increased, I heard the Lord's voice again say, just a little louder,

"Have Jerry pray for you." Again, I was still too embarrassed. I didn't want to impose on Jerry, nor did I want to disrupt the poker game. For several more minutes I lay there in absolute misery. Finally, the poker game broke up and my friends began heading for their separate rooms. I clearly heard the Lord say to me once again: "Have Jerry pray for you."

Whether it was the agony of my pain, desperation, or obedience to the Lord, I called out to Jerry to come to my room. I asked him rather meekly if he would be willing to pray for me. He immediately said, "Sure, no problem," and started praying. As he prayed, I heard the Lord say to me, "Have Jerry lay his hand on you." As Jerry put his hand on my shoulder, I immediately felt this wave of nausea hit me like a ton of bricks. The nausea was overwhelming and I ran to the bathroom with an uncontrollable urge to vomit. Jerry followed me into the bathroom and continued to pray for me.

> What happened next is a mystery to me as well as a miracle.

What happened next is a mystery to me as well as a miracle. The Lord told me to tell Jerry that the hives and nausea were spiritual and that it had to do with my struggle with pornography. I told Jerry that as a little boy my friend and I had found a whole stack of dirty magazines, which began in me an addiction to pornographic images. Even through adulthood, I continued to struggle with this temptation. Jerry started praying for the evil to leave.

The Lord spoke to me again and said: "Remove the pornography." Jerry ran from the bathroom, found the magazine, took it outside and threw it in the trash. When he returned, he started praying with even more confidence and authority.

As he was praying, a deep, dark, gravelly and evil voice inside my throat said, "No, I've had him since he was a little boy. . . . He's mine."

Next, Jerry prayed, "No, he's not yours; he belongs to God! In the strong name and the authority of the Lord Jesus Christ, I command you, spirit of pornography, to leave."

When he prayed this, I felt my whole throat open up and a voice inside me screamed a howl so loud and so awful it was worse than anything I have ever heard in my life. The sound seemed louder than a locomotive, but much more terrifying, and it started deep in my belly and lasted for several seconds. Although my eyes were closed, I could actually see flames leaving my mouth.

Then suddenly, just like that, it was quiet. Both Jerry and I collapsed in a heap on the bathroom floor and wept like little babies. The noise we made was so deafening it woke up all of my friends in the ski lodge. When they came down to investigate, I could actually see the fear in their eyes. I was enraged and I even threatened them, though I don't know why to this day. It was total chaos for almost an hour. My friends took all the silverware in the kitchen and hid it upstairs and did their best to settle me down, and finally we just plain wore out. I must confess that night was one of the strangest nights I have ever endured. I did not sleep the entire night, wondering if I had lost my mind. I could not explain why I had reacted so angrily and out of control. At about 4 a.m., I suddenly remembered the dream I had had a couple of weeks before.

I was so embarrassed. "Why Lord? Why did this happen?" Then the Lord spoke to me. He said, "Spiritual Warfare is real! It's not a game! Satan means business. Satan is preparing businessmen for hell. The love of money is the root of all evil. I wanted to set you free from pornography and from fear! I wanted to reveal My power; I am your tower of strength. Run to Me. I will use you to fill this stadium."

The next morning, my friends sent me packing early. None of them slept much either. They recommended I get some help. I came home, told Therese what had happened and scheduled a meeting with our pastor. We met with Ken Blue at a restaurant and I told him about the dream and what had happened at the ski lodge. I asked him, "Do you think I need to see a psychologist?" Ken answered in a very matter of fact tone, "No, that kind of thing happens all the time." He basically said, "Don't worry about it. God is showing you the truth and setting you free."

It was comforting to know I wasn't crazy, though it took awhile for my friends to agree. But, it was worth the drama to be freed from the grasp of pornography, and to witness firsthand the power of God against the plans of the devil. And, it was worth it to be reminded that spiritual warfare is real and serious.

"And Jesus said to them, I saw Satan fall from Heaven like lightning. Behold, I give to you authority to tread on serpents and scorpions and over all the authority of the enemy. And nothing shall by any means hurt you."

Luke 10:19 (NKJV)

The Lord redeems us from sin, darkness, and hell.

Douglas F. Wall

REDEMPTION

CHAPTER 4

ROMANIA: THE LAND OF ROMANCE

Our church planned a trip to Romania in March 1992, shortly after the fall of Ceausescu and the Communist regime, to preach the gospel and visit orphanages. I have always wanted to travel overseas to learn about other cultures and I was so excited to be traveling across the globe to a country I knew very little about.

In fact, other than Mexico, it would be my first trip to another country. As I stared at the photos of the Romanian orphans, my eyes welled up with tears and I could not understand why I was crying. I didn't even know these children, but tears were flowing from an overwhelming emotion of deep compassion and love.

In preparing for this trip of a lifetime, miracle after miracle occurred. The Lord softened our hearts and showed us the power of prayer, and how delighted He is to answer the most specific prayer request. He expedited my passport and provided my personal funding through over 200 friends and family. He brought in ten times more money than we asked for so we could bring with us additional medical and other supplies for the orphans. Jesus gave me an emotional connection to children I'd never even met, and He showed me firsthand that He could use someone like me, without any missions experience, to change lives and bless others.

Two weeks before we left, as I was waiting to get a haircut, I noticed a homeless man lying on the sidewalk. His wrinkled face and long grey hair and beard told me he had been on the street for a long time. I introduced myself and he said his name was Al. I invited Al to have lunch with me at the fast food restaurant across the street. The manager wanted to throw him out, but I explained that Al was with me. As we sat down together to eat our cheeseburgers, shakes, and fries, Al began to talk with me. As we talked, I looked straight into his eyes. He was born in 1932 and he started drinking in 1944 at the young age of 12. He shared with me that he joined the Army, where he injured his back. He had been married and now he could not find either his sister or his wife. He also shared with me that he hadn't picked up his veteran's check in three months and that he was all alone, without family or friends. I just listened with compassion and grace. I could see his pain and loneliness.

Al allowed me to pray for him. It is said that the eyes are the windows to the soul. I could actually see his eyes light up and come alive as I prayed for him to receive God's forgiveness, redemption, and salvation. I actually could see the Holy Spirit touching his heart. I could also see joy and love come into his eyes. Until that day, I had not witnessed the dramatic and immediate impact my prayers were having on someone. I knew God was preparing me for something very important in Romania.

When our plane landed in Bucharest, Romania, the guards had their AK47 rifles at the ready and the airport was in total chaos, with crowds of people everywhere. Our Romanian hosts drove us from Bucharest to Ploiesti, an oil town approximately two hours away. There were 21 people on our ministry team from three different churches, representing England, Canada, and the United States.

> Until that day, I had not witnessed the dramatic and immediate impact my prayers were having on someone.

As we arrived at the church in Ploiesti that would be hosting our team, we were divided up and introduced to each of our Romanian host families. I was going to be staying with Valeriu and Maria, a young couple in their 20's. I met Valeriu and liked him immediately. Fortunately, on the drive home from the church, our driver spoke English and I was able to communicate with Valeriu. He told me he was a captain in the Romanian army and that he lived in an apartment with his wife, Maria, and they did not have any children. I asked him if he was a Christian and he said no. I asked if he wanted to become a Christian, and he stared at my eyes with hope and joy and immediately said yes!

Our driver dropped us off and as I walked up the long flights of stairs leading to their apartment, I was in awe and wonder at God's blessing for bringing me to this country. I also prayed and asked for God's help to explain the gospel without a translator. As I entered their apartment, Valeriu was so happy and proud to introduce me to his wife Maria and show me around his home. I was so excited and grateful to be right there, right then. The apartment was quite small, a one bedroom, one bath place with a small kitchen and living room. Neither Valeriu nor Maria could speak any English and I could not speak any Romanian, but by the grace of God with the help of the Holy Spirit, and my Romanian-English/English-Romanian dictionary, we were able to communicate quite effectively. We talked for a long time.

Finally, I asked Valeriu if he was ready to be baptized. Although I had never led or performed a baptism before, I took Valeriu, who was still wearing his Romania Army uniform, into the bathroom and, standing with him in the bathtub, I took the shower hose and baptized him into the Kingdom of Heaven. I kept thinking, "How amazing is this?" Afterwards, they were both so excited! Valeriu received a vision of Jesus holding his hand and waving for the entire Romanian army to come to Him. My first night in Romania was quite an experience that I will not forget. We talked for a long time before we finally went to bed.

The next day, our team gathered at the church in Ploiesti. We got on a bus and rode east across the country from Ploiesti to an orphanage in Constanta. Constanta is located on the east coast of Romania, on the west coast of the Black Sea. The bus ride from Ploiesti was several hours and it was fascinating to see the countryside and the horse-drawn carts. It was as if we had time-travelled back a couple of centuries. I can't imagine the countryside would have looked much different then than it did in the moment.

When we arrived at the orphanage, we gathered around outside the building to pray. We didn't really know what we'd find. Walking in the door, we were immediately overwhelmed with the smell of urine and the sound of crying babies. There were only two adults taking care of a hundred children, mostly babies. Many of the babies were crying, pleading to be held and loved. One by one, I watched each of our team members break down and weep as they held and loved these beautiful babies. I was one of the last team members to break down, but then I entered a room filled with disabled children and babies. When they told me that most of the deformities were caused by the fathers beating the mothers when they were pregnant, I was filled with compassion. As I held one of the little boys, I started to cry.

At first, I cried for the little boy because he was crying. Then I cried for that little boy because he didn't have any parents or anyone to hold him. Next, I cried tears of joy that I was not an orphan, and then I cried because I realized how thankful I am that my children are not orphans. And, for the first time, I grieved my daughter Courtney's death. I wept uncontrollably for a long, long time. It was a deep, deep sadness and loss of not being able to hold her, and love her and see her grow up. God was using these beautiful, broken, and abandoned children to begin healing my deep wounds.

Our pastor, Ken Blue, was not immune to the emotion either. I had seen him sitting on the curb outside the orphanage weeping. It was a very difficult and trying experience. In the bus, on the way back, I felt moved to offer to pray for him. We went to the back of the bus and I prayed a short prayer. Afterwards, Ken told me that I'm a natural pastor. Right then and there he ordained me, commissioning me into the Kingdom of God as a priest and pastor for Jesus Christ, in the back of the bus on the way back to Ploiesti.

The next day, my host family, along with a translator, took me up to the mountains of Romania to visit a Romanian Orthodox monastery. On the way up to the monastery, we stopped to pray for a crippled gypsy girl who was missing all of her toes. We were told by one of the locals that it is common for the gypsy fathers to cripple their own children so that they will earn more money begging on the streets. This little girl's eyes were full of anger and hatred and we asked her how old she was. "Seven," she said. She looked like a 60-year-old woman.

At the monastery, we met a young orthodox priest named Stefan. He was 20 years old and very curious because he had not met an American before. He did not speak English but through our translator, was able to give us a tour and explain the sights. We went into a very dark, tall, gothic building enriched with murals and many sacramental objects, including holy icons on the walls. The art, the statues, and the architecture were very dark and I could feel a deep presence of sadness.

As we were walking down the stairs, a very old priest was coming up the stairs toward us. He was wearing the traditional black vestments and black headdress. He looked like he was a hundred years old with his full gray beard and matching gray skin, as well as a big scowl on his face. I asked him if he would allow me to take his picture. Not only did he say no to that, he didn't even want to talk with me. But, I continued my pursuit and asked him if he would let me pray for him. He wanted to know if I was a pastor from America. Because Ken Blue had ordained me the day before, I told him yes and he immediately treated me with respect.

I placed my right hand on his chest and began to pray. Immediately the Holy Spirit fell on him and I could see that he was being touched. He asked if this was black magic. I said, "No, this is the Holy Spirit." He asked again, "Are you sure this is not black magic?" I watched his countenance change as the Lord poured into him His love. The priest was amazed at my enthusiasm. He then let me take his picture and shake his hand. As we said goodbye and I was walking away, I felt compelled to go back and kiss the priest on the cheek. This completely surprised him and he told me I was crazy. I said, "Yes, I am crazy for Jesus." I will always remember the look on his face, and the wonderful laugh that came up from his belly, even changing his skin color from gray to pink. He actually looked 20 years younger and he was still laughing as we left.

As we were preparing to depart for San Diego, eight-year-old Jonathan, son of one of the pastors on our trip, was very sad that we were having to say goodbye. I held Jonathan and the Lord miraculously opened my eyes to sense that He cared for me and was holding me like I was holding Jonathan. I experienced a revelation, there and then, of God's redeeming love. For the first time in my life, I knew with certainty that the Lord is truly with me, crying for me, caring for me, and loving me. He restores my soul.

"He restores my soul; He leads me in paths of righteousness for His name's sake. Yea, though I walk through the valley of the shadow of death, I will fear no evil; for You are with me."

Psalm 23:3-4 (NKJV)

The Lord redeems our brokenness and sorrow and turns our tears into joy and laughter.

Douglas F. Wall

CHAPTER 5

THE EARLY YEARS

I was conceived on New Year's Day 1957—a surprise New Year's baby! I had always heard I was a mistake! It wasn't until much later in life that the Lord revealed to me in a vision His left hand holding my mom's egg and His right hand holding my dad's sperm. And then the Lord put His hands together. This vision has left a lasting impression on me that there are no mistakes in life. God is my Creator and He does not make mistakes!

I was born at Sharp Hospital in San Diego, the second of five children—an older brother Greg, and three younger sisters: Donna, Tammy, and Vicky. My parents met at the Navy Officers' Club in San Diego. My dad was stationed in San Diego and my mom would come to the Officers' Club to meet guys. I remember her telling me stories of how my dad would tease her and at times frustrate her. She said she decided to marry him to teach him a lesson. Although my parents often had a highly vocal way of communicating, I know they truly loved each other.

My sister Donna was born a little more than a year after I was born. She was a beautiful little baby girl with bright eyes and a round, very pretty face. My parents were very happy to have a baby girl—I personally know the challenges of raising boys, and after two, I'm sure a girl was a welcome gift. My mom shared with me years later that there was something very special about Donna.

When Donna was five months old, my dad found her in her crib, not breathing. You can imagine the panic and terror of finding their little baby girl fading away right before their eyes. There really wasn't anything they could do.

According to the SIDS Network, Sudden Infant Death Syndrome is a medical term that describes the sudden death of an infant, which remains unexplained after all known and possible causes have been carefully ruled out through autopsy, death scene investigation, and review of the medical history. SIDS is responsible for more deaths than any other cause for babies one month to one year of age. It strikes families of all races, ethnic, and socioeconomic origins without warning; neither parent nor physician can predict that something is going wrong. In fact, most SIDS victims appear healthy prior to death.

Donna was born on October 28, 1958, and she died on April 10, 1959. She was only 5 ½ months old. My brother and I were just too young to fully comprehend what had happened. I found out from our friend and neighbor Bob, who recalled vividly the day Donna died, how my dad had run over to their home in a total panic calling for Bob's grandma, who was a retired nurse. But, by the time they ran back to the house, it was too late. Bob told me my mom and dad were never the same after Donna's death. How could anyone be the same? Neither one of my parents talked much about Donna. It was a very deep and very painful wound even after decades had passed.

My sister Tamara was born two years after Donna's death. Tammy had beautiful brown eyes, brown hair, and gentle features. My mom bonded to Tammy right away and although Tammy did not replace Donna, the Lord did bring significant healing and redemption through her. As an older brother, I was jealous of my younger sister and teased her, taunted her, and treated her unmercifully. It's a miracle that Tammy doesn't hate me, considering all the mean things I did to her.

My youngest sister Victoria was born in April 1965. She was blonde and blue eyed. I was about 7 ½ years old and remember going to the hospital to see our new sister. Luckily for her sake, I did not see Vicky as a threat and showed her much more compassion and kindness than Tammy.

My dad started his own business in the early 1960's, buying and selling real estate. My dad's business provided for the family; however, at times it was feast or famine. Although as a kid growing up I did not know what the word "escrow" meant,

I did realize that escrow meant we could afford to buy certain discretionary items again.

My brother, sisters, and I were all baptized as babies in the Episcopal Church. My mom would take all of us to church each Sunday. My dad would go to church on Easter and Christmas. Religion was considered important, similar in priority to Little League, Boy Scouts, and music lessons. My mom wanted all of her children to be well rounded and knowledgeable.

I grew up very cynical and skeptical of religion and people in general. As a child, I was always the smallest in the class and I became shy and insecure. I looked to my parents and teachers for approval through my report cards, sports, and doing a good job. I had a terrific childhood but it seemed to go way too fast. I was constantly being told to grow up. I loved being a kid and I found out too soon that it wasn't as much fun to be an adult, with all the added responsibilities. It's very difficult to really appreciate your parents until you grow up yourself and have your own children.

My parents grew up during the depression. *Time* Magazine's cover story in November 1951 identified their generation (born from 1925 to 1945) as the "Silent Generation." The article described this group as "grave, fatalistic, conventional, possessing confused morals, expecting disappointment but desiring faith."

Like many parents of baby boomers, my father didn't talk very much. As a kid, it was awkward to talk to my parents about anything significant. My dad was pretty much shut down emotionally and my mother was too critical to talk to so it was a challenge to have a meaningful two-way conversation with them.

But, one year I was inspired to write a tribute to them for their 40th wedding anniversary.

First (for my own sake and not to share with them), I wrote down all the things that disappointed me about each parent. And then, I forgave them in prayer. Next, I wrote down all the things that I was thankful for and summarized them in a tribute which I had engraved on a plaque along with this wedding photo of them running out of the church.

Here are some excerpts:

A TRIBUTE*

1954 was a year to remember for, on September 12th, Donald Fletcher Wall and Cleo Eleanor Patricia Needham joined in Holy

Matrimony at Trinity Episcopal Church in Ocean Beach. . . . I thank God for both of you and that for whatever reason, you celebrated on New Year's 1957. For nine months later, you had a second mouth to feed, diaper to change and nose to wipe. You probably got sick of looking at messy mouths, poopy pants, and snotty noses. But, you loved us anyway.

There was the time I unscrewed every cabinet in the kitchen . . . the time I climbed into the milkman's truck and broke all of his eggs while you were having coffee . . . and the time I turned the hose into the lawn mower gas tank. Amazingly, you still loved me.

When Donna died, you had to endure a painful tragedy, yet it ultimately made you stronger and you loved all of us more. You taught me how to love and for that I am thankful. Dad, you taught me to love math, to play football and tennis, and to be myself and not to worry about what people think . . . and I believed you. You also taught me that success means more than money and the accumulation of things. Mom, you taught me to love to swim, to tie my shoes, to read and to play chess and you told me that I could do anything if I tried . . . and I believed you. You also taught me the value and importance of family . . .

I remember all the fun family trips to Denver, San Francisco, the zoo, Disneyland, Yellowstone, the snow, camping, Gillespie Pool and the beach. I remember Saint Alban's, Cub Scouts, Boy Scouts, trumpet lessons, art lessons, Little League, swimming lessons, Saturday Night Races, ballgames, and the park. I especially remember Pepper Drive, Cal Metz, the carnival, Rattlesnake Mountain, and all the fun we had growing up.

You helped me to be self-confident, ambitious, and hard-working. You set an example for me of how to be a caring parent and good father. After 40 years you are still setting an example for me. For this I am extremely thankful, because you have shown me how to be a faithful husband and to have a successful marriage. You taught me to have a wife who is also my best friend, for that is what you two are! Best friends!

. . . One more thing you passed on to me is an attitude of giving and serving. You both gave unselfishly to not only your children but many others. You taught me to treat people the way I want to be treated, and to be sensitive and compassionate. You were the perfect parents and I was the perfect son.

You remember the time I ran from the cops, the time I got called into the principal's office, the time Greg and I broke your sliding glass door, the time I wrecked my MG, the times we had those wild parties in your house, the time I hung Tammy upside down in the closet, or how about the time . . . God gave me to you . . . and he gave you to me. I really just want you to know that I love you both very much and I am thankful that I have you. I also want you to always remember that wonderful day in 1954 as you ran out of the church, to reflect on the incredible joy of the moment, and to relive your hope of starting a new family.

Happy 40th Anniversary!
Love,
Douglas

"For You formed my inward parts, You covered me in my mother's womb. I will praise You, for I am fearfully and wonderfully made; Marvelous are Your works, And that my soul knows very well. My frame was not hidden from You, When I was made in secret, And skillfully wrought in the lowest parts of the earth, Your eyes saw my substance, being yet unformed. And in Your book they were all written, The days fashioned for me, When as yet there were none of them."

Psalm 139:13-16 (NKJV)

The Lord redeems our childhood, our innocence, and our childlike faith.

Douglas F. Wall

* Thanks to Dennis Rainey and his book *The Tribute*, Thomas Nelson Inc., ©1994

CHAPTER 6

BORN INTO THE KINGDOM

I was baptized, became an altar boy, and was confirmed at Saint Alban's Episcopal Church in El Cajon, California. From age 13 to 20, I was able to get away with attending church only sporadically. However, we did go to church each year on Easter and Christmas. I did not understand what it meant to have a personal relationship with God but I didn't know what I was missing. The way that I would describe my belief in God was simply that I would go to Him only if I was in extreme need or if I was really desperate.

I started dating my wife, Therese, when I was 20. We would often go to church with her family. Therese was very devout in her Catholic faith. Her father, Bill, loved the Lord and went to Mass and took communion daily. Over the next four years of dating Therese, I became part of their family. On occasion, after Therese would go to bed, Bill would have heart to heart talks with me. We would talk about many things but he loved to talk about Jesus and how Jesus is the son of God and that Jesus was his best friend. I remember thinking to myself, "Wow! He really believes this to be true!"

After graduating from college, I started working for a large accounting firm. The challenges and pressures of a new business career created some serious stress in my life. Social and binge drinking became a pressure release, and with my all-or-nothing personality, I was clearly on a self-destructive path. My life lacked any true purpose, meaning, or direction. I asked Therese to marry me and we became engaged. My drinking grew progressively worse as I desperately tried to relieve my fears, anxieties, and insecurities by abusing my body as well as my mind. This started negatively impacting my relationship with Therese, of course. Finally, the straw broke and she came over to break up with me.

I remember the day as if it were yesterday. I was sitting on the front steps and she gave me back the engagement ring. In the four years we had dated, I had not cried openly with her but on this day I wept. With compassion and unconditional love, Therese started praying for me. The moment she started praying, I remembered my heart-to heart-talks with her father and how he had told me that Jesus is his best friend. At that moment, I knew it was time for me to ask God for help and forgiveness. I put the ring in my pocket, said goodbye to Therese, and drove to a little church in San Diego named Saint Patrick's. On the way to the church, I tried to think about what I would say to God.

As I walked into the empty church, it felt like I had a gigantic backpack of burdens that I was carrying on my shoulders. I knelt down in the very back pew and for the first time in my life, I was prepared to ask God for forgiveness. As I started into my confession, this clear voice that was almost audible spoke and He said: "Doug". It seems ridiculous now but I was so awestruck and amazed that God actually knew my name. I then heard the most healing and redeeming words as He said: "I love you. I forgive you." The Lord spoke to me like a Father would talk to a son. I heard His still small voice tell me to do three things: quit drinking, go back to Therese, and, "Love Me every day." It was a simple conversation, full of grace and mercy, without judgment, without condemnation. That is redemption!

> ...quit drinking, go back to Therese, and, "Love Me every day."

That day was September 25, 1982—three days before my 25th birthday.

When I was a little boy, I always had this strong impression that something important and significant was going to happen before I turned 25. Because God gave me a mathematical mind to understand numbers, I'm very aware when numbers come into play in my life. I can now say with conviction that the Lord has purpose and meaning in all things, including timing.

The Lord is so gracious. He spoke healing into my heart that day and lifted the burden of sin, guilt, and self-hatred. I wept tears of joy and instantly began a new life in Christ. Every aspect of my personality was resurrected in a moment. Redemption, at its very core, is a daily love affair with Jesus.

"And Jesus said to him, 'This day salvation has come to this house.'"

Luke 19:9 (NKJV)

The Lord redeems our very soul.
He is the lover of our soul.

Douglas F. Wall

CHAPTER 7

GOD HEALS AND REDEEMS

In 1983, I went on my first men's retreat with 40 or so other men. It was led by a Franciscan priest by the name of Father Jerry. Father Jerry was blessed with a miraculous gift of healing and the ability to understand God's unique perspective of people and circumstances (called "words of knowledge" in the Bible). He would call men forward with various infirmities and then pray for them to be healed. I immediately noticed how compassionate Father Jerry was and saw his sensitivity to the Lord's leading. He asked the question: "Is there anyone here who was shot in a foreign war?"

Two men came forward. One man had been shot during World War II and the other had been shot during the Vietnam conflict. They looked like tough Marines. I watched in awe and wonder as the Holy Spirit fell on these battle-hardened men as they wept uncontrollably. It was fascinating to me to see God literally take away their pain, suffering, and the trauma of having to endure bullets entering their body. But, the real redemption came when they acknowledged they had inflicted similar wounds upon the enemy. For the Lord wants us to understand His mercy by looking at situations, circumstances and relationships from His vantage point.

Father Jerry then received a word of knowledge that there was someone there that was blind. After he shared that, no one came forward. The ministry team finally translated this into Spanish. Immediately, an elderly Hispanic man came forward. He was completely blind in one eye and partially blind in the other and he looked tired and worn out. Father Jerry told the man that his blindness was the result of a broken relationship from his past. Father Jerry asked the man, "Did you have a relationship that was broken off?" As they translated this into Spanish, the man said, "Si," and nodded his head yes. The old man explained that when he was 20 years old, he had been engaged to be married to a beautiful young woman and he had decided to break off the engagement. Father Jerry asked him what had happened to the young girl. The man started weeping as he confessed that the young girl had committed suicide.

What happened next is both a mystery and a miracle. Father Jerry told this man that it was his guilt that was causing his eyes to go blind. As Father Jerry prayed for Jesus to forgive and remove his guilt, the man looked up with tears of joy as redemption came into his heart and he was able to see again. There were about five or six men with me that watched this miracle and we were all so amazed as we witnessed the healing mercy of Jesus. The Lord heals and the Lord redeems. Blessed be the Lord.

"And Jesus said to him, Receive your sight! Your faith has saved you. And immediately he received his sight and followed Him, glorifying God. And when they saw, all the people gave praise to God."

Luke 18:42-43 (NKJV)

The Lord redeems our authority over blindness, sickness, and sin.

Douglas F. Wall

REDEMPTION

CHAPTER 8

GRACE AND FAVOR

Mother Theresa was born in 1910 in Macedonia, a country in a region with a long history of ethnic and political violence and even genocide. When she was eight, her father – a prominent, middle-class, popular community leader – was murdered by being poisoned for his democratic political beliefs. Her once safe and secure world was shattered and turned upside down, and she watched her mother take on menial tasks for others in order to feed and clothe their family. At the age of 12, she felt the call of God strongly and knew she was destined by God to be a missionary to spread the love of Christ. At 18, she left home to join an Irish community of nuns.

After a few months' training in Dublin, she was sent to India, where on May 24, 1931, she took her initial vows as a nun and committed her life to Christ. From 1931 to 1948, Mother Teresa taught at St. Mary's High School in Calcutta, but the suffering and poverty she glimpsed outside the convent walls made such a deep impression on her that in 1948 she received permission from her superiors to leave the convent school and devote herself to working among the poorest of the poor in the slums of Calcutta. She completely depended on Divine Providence for everything. At first she focused on slum children, and soon she was joined by voluntary helpers. Financial support started coming in, too.

Mother Theresa's life purpose expanded and in 1950, she received permission to start her own order, The Missionaries of Charity, whose primary task was to love and care for those nobody was prepared to look after. Over the years, she received many awards including the 1979 Nobel Peace Prize. The ministry God called her to continues to this day and has expanded all around the globe. Mother Theresa is one of the most recognized and loved people of the 20th century.

I had heard about Mother Theresa. In 1987, just about everyone in the world knew who she was. That year my friend, John Bushnell, and I decided to go down to Mexico once a month to help the poor. We would take food, clothes, and medicine down to wherever the Spirit would lead us. Every time I go to Mexico, my heart breaks as I see great poverty so close to great wealth. This one particular day, John and I loaded up our truck and drove south, eventually winding through the streets of Tijuana. We had received directions to a very poor area that happened to be a place where Mother Theresa's Sisters of Charity provided ministry support. We met up with the director of the ministry and delivered our small load of supplies, for which he was quite grateful. As we were saying goodbye, he mentioned that Mother Theresa would be coming along in about 15 minutes or so and that we were welcome to stay to meet her. Sure enough, about 15 minutes later, a van pulled up near where we were standing. There were no reporters, no entourage, no bodyguards, and no one present but three nuns, Mother Theresa, and us.

I recognized her immediately as she got out of the van, because I'd seen her on television and in photographs and she looked just the same. She was only four feet tall but she was bigger than life. She walked straight to me, grabbed hold of my hands, and looked up into my eyes, as if she were looking right into my soul. As she tenderly held my hands and stared at me with her dark, kind eyes, I felt mercy, compassion, love, and humility pouring out of her. Then she blessed me, and I felt the power of God's love touch me that moment through this tiny woman.

She had an intimacy with God beyond words and spoke with conviction, compassion, and sincerity. Her blessing was simple. The thing that struck me the most is that she spoke with authority. She clearly understood the power and authority of Christ in her. She was unassuming and incredibly humble like a little child. She owned nothing, yet had everything. Mother Theresa at that time was probably one of the most famous and well-recognized persons in the world, arguably the most powerful woman in the world, yet she came right over to me and blessed me like she knew me and we were friends.

I was blessed that day by the Lord. I have often thought about the odds of running into Mother Theresa with no one else around. I don't believe that this was a coincidence or a random meeting. I trust that the Lord orchestrated this divine appointment to bless me with wisdom, grace, and favor. And, just as Mother Theresa blessed me, I was given the opportunity to bless others with wisdom, grace, and favor. Today, this day, I bless you with wisdom, grace, and favor! There are no coincidences in life . . . no random acts, no chance meetings . . . only divine appointments. Every meeting, no matter if it seems trivial and insignificant, is a divine appointment.

"In this life we cannot do great things. We can only do small things with great love."

"The miracle is not that we do this work, but that we are happy to do it."

"We, the unwilling, led by the unknowing, are doing the impossible for the ungrateful. We have done so much, for so long, with so little, we are now qualified to do anything with nothing."

Mother Theresa

"Then the King will say to those on His right hand, 'Come, you blessed of My Father, inherit the kingdom prepared for you from the foundation of the world: for I was hungry and you gave Me food; I was thirsty and you gave Me drink; I was a stranger and you took Me in; I was naked and you clothed Me; I was sick and you visited Me; I was in prison and you came to Me.' "Then the righteous will answer Him, saying, 'Lord, when did we see You hungry and feed You, or thirsty and give You drink? When did we see You a stranger and take You in, or naked and clothe You? Or when did we see You sick, or in prison, and come to You?' And the King will answer and say to them, 'Assuredly, I say to you, inasmuch as you did it to one of the least of these My brethren, you did it to Me.'"

Matthew 25:34-40 (NKJV)

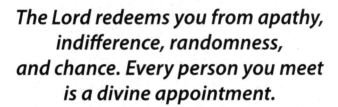

*The Lord redeems you from apathy,
indifference, randomness,
and chance. Every person you meet
is a divine appointment.*

Douglas F. Wall

CHAPTER 9

SWEETIE BOY

The same year I went to Romania (1992), we started home-schooling our oldest daughter, Melissa. Melissa was in first grade and it was a big decision to trust God to help us to lead our children's education. We had several friends that home-schooled their children and we decided to try it out for one year. We were on a path to trust God in all aspects of our lives.

In September 1992, Therese and I found out that she was pregnant. This was our fourth pregnancy. We were elated with joy. We were going to have another baby. Our whole family was so excited! We did not want to find out the sex until the day of delivery. We were scheduled for a C-Section on March 25th but Therese's water broke the night before at 9:30 p.m.

She wrote in the baby book that just as she was going to fall asleep, she rolled over and her water broke. My mom had come over to watch Melissa, Jessie and Scotty. As we left for the hospital, we woke up my mom to let her know that we were going to have the baby.

As we arrived at the hospital, her pants were all wet but she didn't mind, because we were both full of incredible excitement and anticipation. We quickly checked through admissions and they immediately began preparing her for surgery. I also had to wear surgical pants, shirt, shoe and head covers as well as a mask. As I entered the delivery room, the anesthesiologist had already administered the epidural so Therese was feeling no pain. I could feel the excitement in the air and an electricity that is present when you know the Holy Spirit is with you.

As the doctors began to cut into Therese's abdomen, I asked her if she could feel the cutting and all she could feel was a little tugging. Thankfully, the drugs were working just fine. The doctors made quick work in getting the baby out and they pulled out a baby and said. "It's a boy!" Wow! The time was 11:27 p.m. March 24, 1996. We were overjoyed. The joy we experienced was overwhelming. As they cleaned him up and wrapped him in a blanket, my heart leaped for joy as I held him in my arms for the first time. I cried out to Therese: "He is so sweet!" We named him Brent Alexander Wall and nicknamed him "Sweetie Boy."

Later that night, I wrote in my journal: "The baby is beautiful. He has blue eyes and blonde hair. 7 pounds 4 ounces 20 ½ inches and perfect." I got to hold him and we fed him and bathed him. It's great to be a dad. Thank you Jesus!

"This is the day that the Lord has made, let us rejoice and be glad in it."

Psalm 118:24 (NKJV)

The Lord redeems our despair and gives up hope.

Douglas F. Wall

REDEMPTION

CHAPTER 10

IF YOU'VE
LOVED THE
LEAST OF THESE

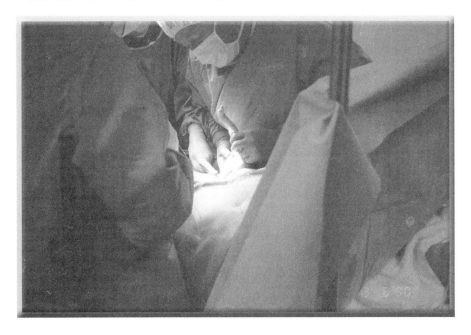

J esus calls us to love babies, the lame, the crippled, the poor, and the least of these. When you love the least of these, miracles happen! I've been blessed with seven wonderful children and all of them are amazing miracles. I would like to share with you the miracle of the birth and life of our sixth child.

Just a few days before Thanksgiving 1994, Therese and I found out that she was pregnant. We were very excited and right from the beginning, Therese knew that this baby was going to be much different than any other baby. She just knew in her spirit, that this child was special. Five months into the pregnancy, we scheduled an appointment for a sonogram.

The initial sonogram was routine and revealed that we were going to have a boy! But, as the nurse continued to scan the womb and check out the baby, she noticed that something was not right. She identified some potential issues and we were told we were going to need to have a more thorough sonogram performed by a doctor considered to be one of the leading experts in her field of reading sonograms. We tried to get some information out of the nurse but she told us not to worry about it. Therese and I were a little concerned about this but that did not prepare us for what happened next.

About a week later, we met with the specialist who conducted a much more sophisticated sonogram that provided a clearer view of our little baby boy. I can still remember the shock and the trauma we experienced upon hearing the doctor's diagnosis. She was very unemotional and matter-of-fact as she explained that our son had several serious birth defects. As soon as she said this, my heart sank into my stomach. She went on to explain that the baby had a hole in his heart, a severe brain defect, a small head, and a left arm that was shorter than the other arm. She told us that our son most likely had "Trisomy 18," a genetic disorder associated with the presence of extra material from chromosome 18. This was later confirmed through amniocentesis.

And then came the biggest bombshell. Because the severity of our baby's condition was incompatible with life, she felt that our son would not survive outside the womb for very long.

She went on to say that the child may or may not survive the term of the pregnancy, but that most definitely he would not live for more than a few days after birth.

This news was devastating and a feeling of despair sank into my soul. I remember praying after our daughter's death that I hoped I would never have to endure another funeral with a 24-inch coffin.

The doctor rather coldly, without emotion or prejudice, asked us if we would like to consider terminating the pregnancy. Her description of the procedure still haunts me. The cervix or womb opening is first paralyzed. Then she would insert a hollow plastic tube with a knife-like tip into the uterus. The tube is connected to a powerful pump with suction much more powerful than a vacuum cleaner. The procedure tears the baby's body into pieces, and the suction vacuums the baby's torn body out of the womb. The placenta is then cut from the inner wall of the uterus and the scraps are also sucked out into a bottle.

> I remember praying after our daughter's death that I hoped I would never have to endure another funeral with a 24-inch coffin.

We declined and knew that the right thing to do was to trust God with our son's life. I have to admit that I was angry at the doctor for suggesting such a horrible procedure. For the next three months we prayed for our son to be healed and we asked our friends to also pray for him. A peace came over us that was clearly supernatural. We decided to name our son Erin, which means "God's Peace."

One night as I was praying, I thought I heard the Lord say to me: "Erin is healed." I was so excited. I told Therese. She was not convinced as she knew that the baby was not kicking her and moving around like her other babies. I was preparing myself for a miracle. Therese was preparing herself for a funeral. We got both.

Therese's water broke a month early and about 30 of our close friends and family showed up at the hospital. I can still remember the excitement and anticipation of witnessing a miracle. The doctors performed a Cesarean section and when they pulled Erin out he was tiny. Everything the doctor had told us about Erin was true. His head was undersized, his left arm was short, his heart was weak, and his body was broken.

But, Erin was a beautiful little boy and he was our son. Our entire family was able to hold him, sing songs to him, laugh and cry with him in our arms. Even our other children — Melissa, Jessica, Scott — were able to see him. Brent was still a baby at that time; however, we all could feel and hear his little heart beating, but it slowly faded during the next 60 minutes as the doctor had said it would. That one hour of our lives seemed to slow down just for us.

We didn't get to see Erin take his first steps. . . . I didn't get to play catch with him or watch him grow up. Many of us know extremely sad stories of men and women that live long lives and yet few if any show up at their funeral. Several hundred people came to our son's funeral. I can still remember the sweet songs, kind words, and the presence of God's love. Later, I asked God a difficult question: "Why would you create a child to live for only 60 minutes?"

He answered me: "I didn't create Erin for 60 minutes. I created Erin to live for eternity. He's healed." And then God put a picture in my mind of what Erin looks like. I saw a full-grown man that looked like the Brawny® man with the mustache on the paper towels.

The world rejects the lame, the crippled, and the least. I honestly can't think of anyone who could possibly be less than Erin—he was definitely in the "least" category. As the doctor had told us, our son's little body was incompatible with life. But, as God revealed to us, if we've loved the least of these, we've loved Christ.

I now understand what Jesus meant when He said this. They say it's important for a father to bond with his child for the first couple of years. I was blessed to hold and love Erin for his entire life. You could also say I bonded with my son for a lifetime. Then I realized that is exactly what God does with us. He bonds with us for a lifetime—and for an eternity.

It was as if God Himself packed all his power and might into the frail little broken body of a child. And, as I held this beautiful little baby, heaven intersected with earth and I knew God had given us a wonderful gift—a miracle. I pray that all of us could experience the miracle of loving the least of these.

Through Erin, God revealed that we should not take any life for granted. Erin's face revealed God's light, beauty, courage, power, grace, and humility. As we held and loved our beautiful little baby, we truly understood the meaning of loving Jesus. We have peace that Erin is completely healed in heaven and we pray that the people we are able to share Erin's story with will also experience the miracle of loving the least.

"In as much as you loved one of the least of these, you have loved Me."

Matthew 25:40 (NKJV)

The Lord redeems us from arrogance, pride, disgust, and disdain for the broken, the poor, the least, the last, and the lost. He pours into us His profound love, grace, humility, compassion, mercy, and kindness.

Douglas F. Wall

CHAPTER 11

SWEETIE GIRL

After Erin's birth and death, Therese and I were apprehensive about having another baby. The Lord knows what's best and Therese was pregnant only three months later. We found out just before Christmas. Surprise! Therese wrote in the baby book: "We found out about you coming along just before Christmas—what a wonderful Christmas present! Mom was so excited and Dad was so proud! The pregnancy went well and without complications but Therese had some anxiety because we just did not know. We went in for a sonogram and they told us were going to have a baby girl and the baby was healthy. We were scheduled for a C-Section on August 5th.

I remember taking Therese to the hospital and the feeling of immeasurable joy. How much more infinite God's joy is for us!

As we both headed into the delivery room, the same sense of excitement and anticipation came over both of us in a way that was very similar to Brent's birth. The birth was a scheduled C-Section and when the doctors pulled her out, we were overflowing with His love. I took one look at her and said she is so sweet. She was born at 1:51 p.m. on August 5, 1996 and we named here Elise Marie Wall. Her nickname became "Sweetie Girl". Later we called her "Leesie."

No one in the family realized how impactful Elise's birth was until we brought her home and her ministry had a significant healing and redeeming anointing on all of us. We missed Erin and we knew he was alive in heaven for eternity but now we had a new little sweetie girl to love, to cuddle, to hold and to kiss. The more we loved her, the more healing we received. Leesie ministered to all of us. We all needed to know that God's hand of mercy and redeeming power was not somehow pulled away. Through Leesie's birth, the Lord gave us abounding evidence that He loves us and is with us. It was truly the icing on the cake.

Our family was now a family of seven children:
Melissa 1986
Jessica 1988
Courtney 1988
Scott 1989
Brent 1993
Erin 1995
Elise 1996

Oh, what a glorious day! God gave us Leesie this day to bring healing, unity and some closure to our family.

"Naked came I out of my mother's womb, and naked shall I return thither: the LORD gave, and the LORD hath taken away; blessed be the name of the LORD."

Job 1:21 (NKJV)

The Lord redeems the broken heart and brings joy and healing to the soul.

Douglas F. Wall

REDEMPTION

CHAPTER 12

HUNTING BEAR

B ear hunting! It sounded adventuresome. It sounded dangerous. It sounded terrifying!

When I first met Nathan Meckel in 1994, I didn't even like guns. The only gun I had ever shot was my dad's little derringer, and it's a wonder I didn't shoot myself in the foot. I was afraid of guns. My mother told me guns were dangerous. What she really meant was that I was dangerous.

Nathan reminds me of a modern day Grizzly Adams. He always has a smile and a story to tell. Most people I know believe their glass is either half empty or half full. Nathan's glass is always running over and spilling out. In 1994 when we met, I was anti-guns, anti-hunting, and anti-killing, yet Nathan convinced me to go with him to a private hunting club ranch just east of San Diego near Pine Valley. The 300-plus acre property, with its rolling hills, oak trees, private lake, and cool breeze, is breathtaking for Southern California.

Nathan took me under his wing and taught me the basics of the outdoor life. He helped me to genuinely appreciate this wonderful and amazing world we live in. He helped me to quiet my soul and listen to the Lord in the wind and the trees. He also helped me to overcome my fear of guns and being alone in the woods.

Through Nathan's leading, my two sons, Scotty and Brent, and I began to gain an understanding and appreciation of gun safety, gun maintenance, and gun storage, as well as when to use caution, how to shoot without flinching, and mostly how to relax and just have fun together. The first time we went to the shooting range, I shot a Winchester 270 high-powered rifle. My son Scotty was only seven and Brent was only four at the time.

One of the first things we learned is what a grouping is. A grouping is the cluster of bullet holes that you have shot on a target. My first grouping at the 100-yard range was the size of a very large platter. I flinched every time I shot the rifle because I was afraid of both the sound and the recoil. Yet, despite my obvious lack of experience, a couple of weeks later, Nathan invited Scotty and me to join him on what would be our first hunting trip. We were going to hunt black bear in Idaho!

I must admit I was nervous! Over the next several weeks leading up to our hunting trip, Nathan actually heightened my insecurity by telling me stories about hunters attacked, mauled, and even killed by bears. I knew he was just teasing and joking around with me, but there was still something about going out into the wilderness to hunt an animal that frightened me. I remember my dad telling me that he went hunting once and he just could not pull the trigger.

It was the first week of May 1997. We took an Alaska Airlines flight from San Diego to Seattle and switched planes to a small prop plane from Seattle to Lewiston, Idaho. Our hunting guide, Ray, picked us up at the Lewiston airport and we were off to Grangeville, Idaho, where we stopped to pick up food supplies, drinks, and some snacks like beef jerky, smoked fish and chips, etc. Next, we stopped at the local sporting goods and hunting supply store to pick up the bear tags and hunting licenses that Ray had already secured for us. I can tell you that I have never seen a store like this in California! It was incredible! We purchased some ammo and other supplies and then headed about an hour up the mountain.

The Lord had delivered a snowstorm the week before but it was melting fast. As we left town, I remember feeling excited, and a little bit anxious, but it was so beautiful. Winding up the long, two-lane road, we saw whitetail deer, Canadian geese, and awesome scenery. The river was running fast from the snow runoff and our guide had an endless supply of stories about steelhead fishing. But, we weren't coming all this way to go fishing! We were hunting bear! I looked at Scotty and realized that he was just as excited as I was. This was going to be quite the adventure!

As we arrived at the top of the mountain ridge, we could see forest forever! The trees were a deep gorgeous green, the sky was clear and bright, and the freshness of the air was invigorating. The sun was just going down and we could see to the west a spectacular and colorful sunset. We left the road at the top of the ridge and drove down a dirt road approximately one mile to our beautiful log cabin. We immediately unpacked, put on our camouflage gear, and loaded up for some pre-dusk bear hunting.

Scotty was too young to have a gun, but he was very comfortable being with me and observing. We drove about five miles from the cabin, parked the car on the side of the road, and started hiking down to the place where the guide had put down bear bait earlier that day. He explained to us that bears have very keen senses of smell and hearing so it was important that we stay upwind and be extremely quiet. By the time we arrived near the bait, it was just starting to get dark. We came upon a slight clearing and peeked cautiously approximately 130 yards down the hill to the bait, and spotted a huge black bear. Ray, our guide, asked me to rest my Winchester 270 rifle on a fallen log that was hanging at a forty-five degree angle from a tree down to the ground.

As Nathan and Ray were whispering about how to move all of us closer to the bear, I decided to look through the riflescope to see if I could get the bear in my sights. Nathan and Ray continued to whisper instructions because they wanted to help me to make the shot since I was such a rookie. I was totally oblivious to their conversation, though, or what was happening. I was completely in my own world, zeroing in on this bear through my scope. I was crouched down trying to get comfortable and at the same time steady the rifle on the fallen log. The more I fidgeted, the more the log would move and the less comfortable I was. Finally, I got my rifle secure and my nerves calmed down. I was now eyeing this huge black bear in my crossbar sights. The light was slowly turning into darkness and my heart was throbbing like a drum. I tried to remember all the things that I was coached on, such as the key to shooting a bear is to shoot just below the shoulder. Bears have very thick hides, so thick they have been known to take a shot and not even feel it or be fazed by it.

I became so focused that Nathan and Ray did not exist. They were completely shut out of my thoughts and awareness. I quietly took the gun safety off and took a deep breath in. My heart was now pounding as if it was exploding in my chest, but ever so slowly I exhaled. Time stood still for what seemed an eternity . . . and I gently squeezed the trigger.

I did not hear the sound of the gun going off. Do you know just how loud a high-powered rifle is in the middle of a quiet forest, especially when you are not expecting it? I had neglected to tell Nathan or Ray that I was going to shoot. They were both caught completely off guard and the gunshot scared the you-know-what out of them both. When you are hunting with others and you are ready to take the safety off, you're supposed to let other hunters know that you're preparing to shoot!

After I pulled the trigger, I couldn't see anything. None of us saw what happened to the bear, but we could all see that he was no longer standing, or lying, down by the tree. We had no idea if the bear was dead, wounded, or if I had simply missed.

After Nathan and Ray recovered from their shock, they yelled at me for scaring them so badly. They decided that Scotty and I should stay where we were and that they would go down and find out what had happened to the bear. There is very little natural light in the woods at night, and Nathan and Ray took off, leaving me all alone in the middle of nowhere with Scotty. Keep in mind, this was our very first hunting trip as well as our very first time out in the forest, and now we were on our own. Just to be safe, I must have checked my gun to make sure it was loaded a dozen times. This was by far one of the most intense and yet peaceful moments of my life. Yet, I kept thinking, it's now pitch black and that bear's coming back to find revenge because I tried to shoot him!

It's amazing how active and sensitive all of our senses become when our bodies are on high alert. Every sound in the forest is magnified—every drop of a twig or whisper of wind. I can still smell the bark and needles of the pine trees. I remember how quickly Scotty's and my eyes adjusted to the darkness, and even how relatively comfortable with the darkness we became. For the next hour, we faced the growing realization, both exhilarating and terrifying, that we were not alone in this wilderness. Thankfully, we couldn't see what else was out there! When Nathan and Ray finally came back, they told us they had tracked the bear quite a ways and that my shot had nicked him. We all went back to the cabin, and I felt terrible about what had happened. I learned a very important lesson that night. If I am going to take a shot at an animal, I need to be highly confident in my shot.

The next day, Nathan and Ray coached me and we practiced target shooting. I was very focused on learning this time, how to steady the rifle on a solid log, how to zero in on the target, and how to not flinch as I slowly squeezed the trigger. With some serious help from Nathan and Ray, I started to gain confidence and was able to improve my groupings within four inches.

As evening approached, we headed out to the bait and got there early. We had approximately three hours of light left. I was so proud of Scotty, who patiently waited and was as quiet as a mouse for three straight hours, whittling sticks with his pocketknife. That evening we saw a mama bear and her two cubs—beautiful animals. I was happy just to watch them and admire these incredible creatures created by God. I made a decision that evening that I was never going to take the shooting of an animal lightly again.

On the third night, another guide, Daryl, joined us and we went to a completely different place. We were able to get there a couple of hours before dark and Daryl, Scotty, and I settled into our spot overlooking the bait. (Nathan and Ray went to a different location.) We were able to set up our rifles approximately 100 yards from the bait upon a very firm and solid stump. A small, male, black bear came into view, but after studying it through my binoculars, I decided to wait. As that bear took off, a much larger bear approached the bait. I scoped out this larger bear for a long time. Looking through the riflescope, I placed the bear's shoulder right in the center of the cross hairs. For what seemed like an eternity, I watched this large and beautiful animal and wondered if I should shoot. I remembered how bad I felt the first night and I did not want to make that mistake. As I continued to study the bear, a peaceful confidence came over me, and the bear turned sideways as if to give me a very clear shot. I steadied the rifle and told Daryl and Scotty that I was taking the safety off. As I lined up the crosshairs just below the shoulder, I took a deep breath. My heart was thumping but not nearly as much as the first night. I slowly breathed out and squeezed the trigger.

This time my shot hit the bear in the perfect spot. The bear was dead immediately. Daryl told me to take a second shot to be safe. As Daryl, Scotty, and I walked the 100 yards down to where the bear lay, we approached with caution. It did not dawn on me until I came up to this very large dead animal lying there on the ground, the emotions I was feeling. I felt joy as well as sadness at the same time. I realized right then how precious life is.

There is a wise old saying that goes, "Something must die in order for something else to live." Every bite of food we eat, whether it's a wheat kernel, a chicken leg, or bear meat used to be alive. Food is essential to sustain life. Death is not something to take lightly. Life is precious!

On the fourth night, Scotty and I were able to go hunting with Nathan. As we waited patiently, a doe and her fawn came within 20 feet of us and because we were downwind they could not smell or hear us. It was wonderful to watch and observe these beautiful wild animals so close. I finally began to listen. My mind and my ears were finally adjusting to the quiet of the forest. The noise of life and all its anxieties faded away and I could hear the wind whistling in the trees. I could hear the sound of squirrels as they chased each other; I could hear the sweet sounds of birds as they sang their songs. It was as if the Lord was playing a musical symphony just for me. I will never forget the peaceful sound of the forest revealing the awe and wonder of God's creation.

It was an incredible trip, a trip Scotty and I will remember for the rest of our lives. We saw elk as large as cars crashing through trees. We saw wild turkey flying through the forest flashing with their red, white, and brown feathers. We saw these beautiful mule deer and white tail deer grazing and prancing about. The Lord revealed Himself and His amazing creations in so many ways. Scotty and I gained a tremendous love and appreciation for the wilderness with all of its beauty. But, the greatest revelation from God, was our new and growing heartfelt love and respect for life. Life is precious in every way. We will not take it for granted.

As we were leaving the mountain and coming back down the hill to Grangeville, I looked over at Scotty and saw that he was crying. I asked him what was wrong. Was he feeling ill? Was he homesick? He looked up at me with tears in his eyes and said to me, "I don't want this trip to end!"

"And David said, the Lord who has delivered me out of the paw of the lion and out of the paw of the bear, He will deliver me out of the hand of the Philistine."

1 Samuel 17:37 (NKJV)

The Lord redeems our courage and boldness. He also gives us an appreciation for His creation even when faced with our powerlessness in nature.

Douglas F. Wall

CHAPTER 13

RUNNING
WITH JESUS

Whenever you are about ready to embark on change, it can be an exciting time as well as a stressful time. Whether you are running a business, traveling abroad, starting a new semester at school, or just getting married, life is full of change, which can bring on anxiety and fear. Fear can be our number one enemy. Fear comes in many forms. Some fears bring about terror and horror. Some fears are paralyzing. Other fears are just annoying. One thing is certain: fear is an emotion that has a powerful impact on our mind and our health. Fear, anxiety, worry, and stress can be deadly and play a contributing role in the majority of heart attacks, strokes, ulcers, and infectious disease.

Running a business is a recipe for stress and fear because change is a constant. As a business owner, at times I feel strongly that all the challenges and burdens of the company are heaped on my shoulders.

When a friend of mine and I started our first business in 1985, we provided management consulting services to small companies.

The name of our firm was RCG Management, which stood for Resource Consulting Group (RCG). Our goal was to be a resource for emerging growth companies. Initially, we provided financing and accounting management primarily to start-up and early stage companies. Early on, it was both exciting and fun to run our own business. As we expanded and provided Chief Financial Officer services, Human Resources management services, information systems and integration services, marketing and business planning services, and interim CEO services, the business grew and we hired employees. As our network of resources as well as our employee count expanded, our client base also expanded. We served a broad range of businesses from start-ups to Fortune 1000 companies. Our company developed a diverse management service offering to both private and public companies.

For the next 16 years, we grew from two employees to over 100 employees and served over 1,000 clients. Because of the number and diversity of our client base, we had to deal with some very intense conflicts and sometimes difficult and stressful situations.

Additionally, we had to make sure we always had enough cash in the bank to make our payroll. Two payrolls every month for 16 years is a lot of payrolls for a small business, especially for a business that served cash-strapped start-ups and emerging companies. Additionally, one of our roles as CFO was to help our clients make their own payrolls. There was never a dull moment at RCG! One of RCG's roles in serving our clients was to be a sounding board/sanity check. I loved what my dear partner Bill used to say so often to his clients, "I never made a mistake until someone checked my work."

At RCG, we saw and dealt with a diverse number of issues including employee theft, management embezzlement, IRS fraud, bank fraud, investor fraud, management drug and alcohol addiction, illegal activity, Board of Director conflicts, hostile takeovers, family fighting, lawsuits, IPOs, venture capital transactions, etc. Our firm was right in the middle of very intense and often volatile situations.

Because we were contracted consultants and not full-time employees, we would often be in a superior position to provide objective and impartial counsel. Additionally, I believe our clients were more likely to receive and accept our counsel than if our consultants were working full-time on our client's payroll. The reason for this is that our consultants were for the most part independent professionals and not necessarily controlled by any one person or client. I am so grateful as I reflect on how the Lord miraculously helped us to serve our clients with all of those complex and difficult issues as well as how we successfully made every single payroll. Now that is the grace of God!

In order to help deal with all of this work-related stress, I started to train for triathlons (swimming, biking, and running). Every Tuesday, I would meet my good friend Stan at lunch and we would run from Torrey Pines State Beach up on the cliffs to Del Mar and then come back along the beach. Stan and I called this four-mile run our "beach loop."

Stan and I decided early on to invite Jesus to run with us. We would take turns unloading all of our problems, challenges, and issues on each other and Jesus and by the following Tuesday, every single issue and problem was miraculously solved. This happened so many times that I lost count! We always looked forward to running together because we knew that Jesus would be there running with us and giving us wisdom, insight, and clarity.

On one of our first runs, Stan shared with me how frustrated he was at work because he did not have a very good relationship with his boss. He told me that his boss didn't listen to him and when he tried to talk with him, he felt intimidated. At the end of our run, the Lord put it on my heart to encourage Stan to pray for his boss. We stood in the Torrey Pines parking lot and prayed. Stan committed to pray for his boss and renounced his fear of this man.

The following Tuesday, Stan was visibly excited when we met for our run. He told me that he had started praying for his boss like I had encouraged him to do. The next day he was working late in the office—everyone had gone home except him and his boss. He happened to walk by his boss's office and his boss looked up from his desk and yelled at him with intimidation and intensity, "What are you still doing here?"

Because Stan had been praying diligently for this man, he looked his boss right in the eye and yelled back with confidence and intensity, "Because I want to be!"

His boss started laughing and they had a great talk for the first time. The next day, his boss invited him to his house for a party the following Friday. From that point on, Stan's relationship with his boss completely changed and they actually became close friends. To this day, over 18 years later, Stan and his former boss are still very close friends. This is the truth. There is great power in loving others through prayer, which conquers fears, our anxieties, and our stress.

"Listen to me, you who know righteousness, you people who have my law in your hearts: Do not fear the reproach of men or be terrified by their insults. For the moth shall eat them like wool; but my righteousness shall be forever, and My salvation from generation to generation."

Isaiah 51:7-8 (NKJV)

The Lord redeems you from the fear of men and the anxieties of this world. The beginning of wisdom is the fear of God.

Douglas F. Wall

REDEMPTION

CHAPTER 14

FINISHING STRONG

My buddy Stan convinced me to train for and complete my first marathon. I knew that Stan had completed several Ironman triathlons and that he had run full marathons (26.2 miles) after swimming 2.4 miles and cycling 112 miles. Stan inspired me and I decided to do some historical research on marathons.

According to historians, the very first marathon was inspired by the tale of Philippides, a speedy runner who was said to have run from the plain of Marathon to Athens in 490 BC to convey the news that the Athenians had defeated the Persians. Apparently, this very first marathon was no easy task. It is said that when Philippides finished the run, he gasped, "Be joyful, we win," and then dropped dead of exhaustion.

This is not a very comforting beginning for the history of marathons. Apparently, Philippides' death has been the inspiration for millions of people who seem to want to kill themselves ever since.

I signed up for the Carlsbad, CA Marathon and began training. The secret to training for a marathon is to not try to do too much too fast. Just like eating an elephant one bite at a time, training for a marathon is a slow and gradual climb to the 26.2 mile run. It's a good idea to keep a running diary and track your weekly runs, being careful not to increase your distances more than 10% from the previous week.

My longest training run leading up to the marathon was 17 miles. We ran from the UTC area of San Diego all the way to La Jolla and back. I felt pretty strong on that run, but I was also tired.

The night before the marathon, I was so excited I could not sleep. I arrived over two hours before the race was to begin. It was still dark and I had butterflies in my stomach. I met Stan and we stretched, drank some Gatorade, and mentally prepared ourselves for the run. The time leading up to the race seemed to slow down and take forever. You know that you are in that moment when time stands still and your life is never going to be the same.

The sun came up and it was a beautiful day. As the start of the race drew close, you could feel the runners' excitement and energy levels increase. The atmosphere was charged! I was excited and ready to go when the buzzer finally went off. Stan had warned me not to go out too fast. We kept to our running pace and I felt surprisingly strong after the first 13 miles. Five miles later, when I hit mile 18, I remember thinking to myself, 'Wow, this is the longest run of my life!' And then this thought came into my head . . . 'I still have over eight miles to go!' At that moment, I became mentally and physically defeated and all the adrenaline and extra energy storehouse was spent.

There was an ice cream stand at mile 18 giving away small vanilla ice cream cones. Stan tried to get me to eat one of those cones but the thought of ice cream made me nauseous. My stomach was empty. I was completely out of fuel and I still had eight miles to go.

I toughed it out for the next two miles and when I hit mile 20 I wanted to quit. Stan kept pushing me so I dug out another two miles and when I hit mile 22 I hit the wall.

"Hitting the wall" in a marathon is that place where physical, mental, and spiritual exhaustion overwhelms you to the point where you have no more glycogen reserves. Glycogen is the substance stored in the muscles and liver that provides the primary fuel the muscles need. Carbohydrates produce glycogen. At the time, I did not know any of this. I just knew I was finished.

As I arrived at the aid station at mile 22, I collapsed into a chair and told Stan I was done. Now, I could see why Philippides had collapsed and died. My calves and my quadriceps were so sore and full of lactic acid I was totally exhausted. Part of me thought I had died. I still had four more miles to go but with an empty tank I wasn't going anywhere. Stan kept trying to get me to eat something. For the next 10 minutes I sat there in the shade of the aid station tent while Stan continued to encourage me to eat something. Finally, he convinced me to have a small bite of a Snickers bar.

I kid you not, just like those hilarious commercials, within a few minutes of eating that small bite of Snickers, the Lord redeemed strength and hope into my body and my mind. Suddenly, I had confidence that I could actually finish this marathon. My attitude changed from defeat to victory and I told myself, "It's only four miles." "One mile at a time," I just kept saying to myself. Stan was my encourager and the Lord is my redeemer! Stan kept telling me that Jesus was running with us. Stan would run ahead and use the orange construction cones as a megaphone, yelling to the crowd, "And here comes Doug Wall, superstar runner and marathoner." I must admit he looked ridiculous out there yelling my name but the Lord was using Stan to motivate me, encourage me, and keep me going. It was working!

> My attitude changed from defeat to victory and I told myself, "It's only four miles. One mile at a time."

As I finally arrived at mile 25, I knew I was going to finish. I could actually taste the end of the race. Like a horse that can smell the barn, I became confident, ignoring the screaming pain in my legs and focusing on the goal ... to finish and to finish strong. Stan continued to encourage me and lift up my spirits, but what was really impressive were the crowds of people cheering me on. The last mile was filled with fans and bystanders on both sides of the street clapping, yelling, and cheering. Their faces said it all: Compassion, love, and joy!

"We are proud of you."
"Way to go."
"You can do it."
"You're almost there."
"Keep going."
"We love you!"

As we got closer and closer to the finish, the roar of the crowds got louder and louder. I was feeding off of the energy level all around me and it was both contagious and intoxicating. I can remember how the cheers actually impacted my attitude and my energy level. My heart and soul soared and adrenalin that I did not think I had kicked into gear. When I turned the corner and could actually see the finish line with the balloons and the banners about 300 yards ahead, I felt power and strength surge into my body. I actually increased my running speed and I knew that victory was mine!

There are moments in your life that stay with you forever. This was clearly a moment I will never forget. Time stood still in this moment as I crossed the finish line. I could feel the tears well up in my eyes. I had never felt so good. The combination of the thrill of victory and the relief of agony was mind numbing. It was such an amazing feeling. I will treasure this moment in time for the rest of my life, even though I have since competed in and completed a number of marathons and triathlons.

I persevered. I did not quit. I overcame. I finished strong!

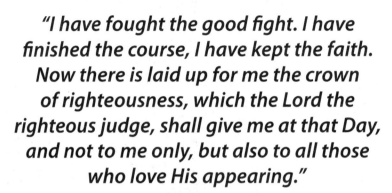

"I have fought the good fight. I have finished the course, I have kept the faith. Now there is laid up for me the crown of righteousness, which the Lord the righteous judge, shall give me at that Day, and not to me only, but also to all those who love His appearing."

2 Timothy 4:7-8 (NKJV)

The Lord redeems you from giving up and He gives you His strength to finish strong.

Douglas F. Wall

CHAPTER 15

RETURNING TO ROMANIA

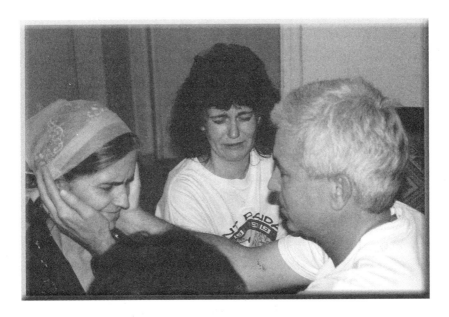

In 2001 I made plans for a second visit to Romania, the "land of romance," with a team of old and new friends and 40,000 pounds of food and supplies. After nine years, I was very excited about returning to the place where the Lord had showed me His healing and forgiveness. We were scheduled to leave on Tuesday, September 12, 2001. My wife, Therese, frantically woke me up the morning of September 11th with the news about the attack on the Twin Towers. We were in shock and disbelief as we watched the television all day. Our team gathered that evening to pray for our country and to reconsider our Romania trip, which didn't seem very important in comparison to the grieving all of us were experiencing. Though the tragic events left many of us feeling insecure and fearful, as we prayed, we felt compelled to put aside our fear and trust in God's guidance and protection.

The very first international flights after 9/11 did not leave San Diego airport until September 16th. The next day, September 17th, we were very fortunate to be able to get on the second British Airways flight from San Diego to London. When we arrived in Bucharest, the capital city of Romania, the weather was balmy, almost tropical. We loaded all of our boxes and bags into the bus and headed for our host church in Ploiesti, approximately one hour north of Bucharest. Our team, now 18 in number (and there were others who helped coordinate the shipment), gathered in the church sanctuary for prayer and worship before dispersing to our host families. We gave thanks to the Lord for a host family that had received salvation the day before, for our travel safety, and for the opportunity to serve in this beautiful country of Romania. It warmed our hearts as numerous people thanked us for coming and told us they were praying for America.

The morning of our first full day, we drove to a home for the elderly that housed 110 men and women. As we walked from room to room, we sang worship songs and prayed for each precious soul to receive the love of Christ. Looking into the eyes of one of the women, I could actually see the love of God shining back at me and knew I was supposed to be there. Tears filled my eyes and I was overwhelmed with joy and peace to be right there at that place at that time. This is one of those moments I will always treasure.

Back in Ploiesti (our "hometown") for lunch, we celebrated pastor George's birthday. George was the pastor of the church that our

Romanian hosts attended. After the party, we headed to the church for a service of worship and ministry. Ken Blue spoke on God's grace and that there is no condemnation for those who are in Christ. After the teaching, people were invited to come forward for prayer. A young gypsy boy who had contracted AIDS came forward. I asked the little boy if he had received Jesus in his heart. He said: "Yes, just now!" We prayed for the Lord to heal him not just spiritually but physically as well. We were all touched by this little boy's smiling face revealing a new and everlasting joy.

We visited a small gypsy church in Ploiesti on the second floor of an old building. The service began and incredibly beautiful Romanian music filled the church with a sad but tender love. There were approximately 75 people in the church that night. I was told that many of the men were not in church because it was grape harvest time. Ken spoke about the prodigal son and the love of the Father. Afterward, we invited people to come forward so that we could pray for the sick.

A little boy named Stephan came forward. One of his legs was crushed in a fall and he couldn't walk very well. His eyes were foggy, dark, and filled with despair. I asked him if he believed that this accident was God's judgment on him. He said da (yes), reflecting many Romanians' belief that God has cursed Romania. We prayed for Stephan to receive God's mercy and forgiveness. We prayed for Jesus to take away judgment and condemnation and for him to be set free. We explained to him that in the book of James, God tells us that mercy triumphs over judgment. I looked into Stephan's eyes and they changed from dark and despondent to clear and sparkling. I was totally amazed as I could see how the Lord had filled him with new hope, love, and joy. He excitedly told us he was overjoyed and said his legs felt much better.

We traveled with the team to Sinaia in the Carpathian Mountains to see a castle and do some touring of the countryside, appreciating the rich and amazing beauty of Romania. The fresh air and scenery were spectacular. We were given a tour of a castle and then we headed to a small mountain church. Pastor George started talking to an older woman in the back of the church. He asked me if I would pray for her as she had been suffering from severe headaches. As we talked with the woman, we found out that she believed that her headaches were God's judgment of her.

We asked Jesus to remove judgment, condemnation, and fear, and to break the power of any curses that had been inflicted on her, including her own self-inflicted curses. Within a few minutes of prayer, her headaches were completely gone. She was so grateful to the Lord! She told us that she had been in such agony from her headaches that she had prayed to God to send someone to pray for her, and then we showed up. All we could say is Praise God! He works in mysterious ways!

One morning after visiting another church, I began to feel very ill. I asked the team for prayer and as several team members prayed for me, I received the following vision:

I was at the bottom of a 200-foot well. The only light was a pinhole straight up. The well was dark, polluted with foul oil and gas and it smelled like death. I looked up and saw WWII bombers raining bombs down on the city. As the bombs hit, fires broke out everywhere. It smelled like burning oil and gas. The stench was unbearable. I couldn't breathe. I looked down and saw a dead baby that had been tossed into the well. The baby's face was stark white yet innocent and beautiful. I realized that death had polluted the well water causing the water to be unsafe to drink. I asked the

Lord how to pray for the healing of the baby as well as cleansing of the water. The Holy Spirit revealed to me how to pray: Ask for God's light, salt, water, and blood. As I prayed, I could first see the Lord's love and light shining down into the well and removing every shadow and all darkness. Next, I saw the Lord's tears raining down and bringing cleansing. Finally, I saw the Lord's blood streaming down into the well, bringing forgiveness, freedom, and redemption.

The next day, I woke up with a cold and stuffy head. I asked Jesus to heal my body, my lungs, and my head. I asked Him to heal my immune system. I prayed for strength that day, because we were going to visit an orphanage with approximately 50 toddlers. As we arrived, I was reminded what a blessing it is to visit an orphanage. We held these beautiful children and laughed and cried and played with these kids for hours. This was a very special time for the entire team. We were all blessed. We prayed for the staff and for the director and felt the love of God powerfully as we prayed. We came to give and received so much more.

Next, we went into town and shared Jesus with a man on the street. He received our prayers. We gave him some money and told him where our host church was. Later that evening, the man showed up at the church. I was scheduled to speak on the local Christian radio station, but I started to get a very high fever and infection in my lungs. We went home and called the doctor. My fever continued to rise and I was having severe asthma symptoms. I remember this thought kept coming into my mind that I could actually die in Romania that night! To counter that thought, I began praying to Jesus: "I give you my life tonight." Thankfully, as I was praying, Neil, one of our team members, showed up and began praying for me. As he started to pray, I told him to speak with the authority of Jesus and tell illness and evil to leave.

The vision of Romania continued and I saw the baby that was thrown down into the well. The baby represented new life, the next generation, and the new church. The people in the well with me were terrified. You could not see any light unless you looked straight up, but no one was looking up. The shame was so intense, the people could only look down. The churches of Romania were apathetic, filled with hate and fighting, back-stabbing and false accusations. The churches were unable to help or pray for the dead child. They were filled with unbelief and lacked any compassion or care.

The Holy Spirit showed me the churches and their need to reconcile, unite, and ask God for forgiveness. I prayed for church unity and reconciliation and as I prayed, I saw the well open up and the light of Christ shine down into the well. The tears of Christ came down and brought cleansing to the church, to the water, and to the baby. Then I saw the blood of Christ come down the sides of the well and begin to pour over the church. I saw the church (orthodox, Pentecostal, Catholic, Baptist, and every denomination) begin to pray and sing together and ask God for forgiveness. I saw them gathered around the dead baby and I asked the Lord to resurrect the child. The love of the Lord filled the place as the well was cleansed of darkness, unforgiveness, and death. Then suddenly and miraculously, I saw the child's eyes begin to change from death to life. The church gathered closer, holding hands around the baby, and sang and worshipped the Lord together and then I saw the most amazing thing! The baby actually came back to life! Everyone was overwhelmed with joy. They were dancing and filled with awe and wonder.

Two doctors came during the prayer time with Neil. They were amazed at how my health and color had changed during the 30 minutes or so that Neil prayed for me. They gave me a shot the size of a samurai sword that kept me awake the whole night. I prayed the entire night, thanking God for the vision and asking Him to use me to help bring the power of redemption to the least, the last, and the lost. From that point on, I was filled with a new confidence and peace and prayed with much more boldness and authority.

One day we drove to a small village called Gaesti and met with Kathleen, who works with a small church that has a ministry to street children, and specifically, rescuing young girls from being kidnapped into slavery and forced prostitution. We gave Kathleen several boxes of soap, shampoo, toothpaste, toothbrushes, makeup, feminine napkins, and medical supplies. We also brought with us rent money for six months, and six sewing machines along with thread and sewing supplies to help Kathleen get the girls started in a sewing business of their own. They were so happy and blessed that Kathleen and many of the girls cried with tears of joy.

Kathleen was caring for 32 teenage girls that she had rescued from the orphanage and from the street. Each of the girls is so beautiful and childlike and filled with curiosity. We could tell that Kathleen had already made a significant impact on their lives in the short time since she had taken them in. We could immediately see that she loved each of them like they were her very own children. We were able to meet and pray for each of these special daughters. Many of the girls were shy but each one had a very sweet spirit and we asked the Lord to continue to reveal His amazing grace and healing to them. As I prayed for these girls, my heart was filled with both sadness for their past as well as joy for their future. I asked Jesus to bring comfort from the pain and hurt of not having either a loving father or mother, and I asked God to fill their hearts with joy because Jesus has come to take the place of their parents and to give them a new future. We cried as we prayed for each of these precious girls, some of whom had been particularly wounded. We were all very moved by the Lord's love for each of these children.

Back at Kathleen's home, we gathered in a small church at the back of the property to give thanks to our awesome and amazing Lord and praise Him for everything. The room was smaller than a living room and filled with families and many of Kathleen's little girls. I sat right in the middle and, as we sang songs both in English and Romanian, the love of Jesus filled the room and it was such an incredible experience.

A very sweet little boy stood and sang a beautiful love song to the Lord and I couldn't help but weep as it touched my soul. The words were Romanian but the song was so moving and filled with the Holy Spirit, we could understand every word. After worship, we invited anyone who needed prayer to come forward. Our team prayed for many people, and we witnessed many miracles as Jesus, in His generous love and grace, touched and healed people. One woman had severe heart problems that had begun when her husband died a few years earlier. We prayed for her and watched the sorrow and grief of her husband's death lift off of her, changing the color of her face and clearing the grief from her eyes. Seeing her sorrow turn to joy, we thanked Jesus.

A little eight-year-old boy with severe recurring headaches came forward. The boy didn't speak any English so we used a translator. We asked him when the headaches began and he told us that they started when he was very little and there was an accident and he fell. As we began to pray for him, the Lord told us that it wasn't an accident. We asked him what had really happened and the boy told us that his father had thrown him against a wall. My heart broke for the boy and we both started to weep. We sobbed for the intense pain of having a father who would intentionally hurt his child. We asked Jesus to give the boy forgiveness for his father, and though he wasn't there to receive it firsthand, his son took the giant step of forgiving him and our sadness turned to joy. And suddenly, the boy's headaches left and he was completely healed. We both were filled with wonder and amazement. Jesus truly loves His children and that is the greatest joy. Forgiveness is so powerful!

A young woman came forward who had recently lost her daughter. The young mother had beautiful but very sad eyes and didn't speak English. The pastor translated for me, and I found out her daughter's name was Emma and she was only four years old. A speeding car had killed her little girl right outside that very church just a short time before. I saw the sorrow and pain of losing a child and I began to cry for her. I saw that Jesus was crying for her. As I started to pray for her, the Lord reminded me of when my daughter Courtney had died. I remembered how guilty I had felt for being away when she died. I had felt like it was my fault for leaving that weekend. I had falsely blamed myself for Courtney's death and I remember feeling I deserved this punishment and suffering because I had thought I was not a good enough father.

I heard this still small voice say to me: "It's not your fault." As I told her this, holding back my own tears, she began to sob uncontrollably. I told her that Jesus takes her sorrows and pain. I told her that He takes the blame from you and He takes the blame for you. We both cried for a very long time and then I asked Jesus to take away her self-condemnation and self-criticism and bless her with the grace to accept the fact that this accident was not God's judgment or punishment of her. I told her how much Jesus loves her and that He trusts her and wants to give her more of His love. I saw her face change as I asked Jesus to fill her with peace and comfort.

A wonderful peace came over the church and the woman's eyes became clear and filled with love. Jesus gave us a wonderful gift that day. I thanked Him over and over.

The last orphanage we visited housed children aged six years to 18 years who had mental and physical disabilities. As soon as I walked into this orphanage, all I could think about was that it was an awesome birthday present as that day I turned 44. We saw 60 children all sitting down very quietly and the moment seemed awkward. But, suddenly we ran down each of the aisles slapping high-fives and hugging each of the kids, and the place erupted into laughing and shouts of joy and clapping. Many of the children had burns, scars, deformities, crippled hands, crippled legs, mental illness, and sicknesses. We asked Jesus to bring healing and blessing on each of the children. We sang songs, worshipped the Lord and blessed every one of these beautiful kids. We prayed and laid hands on each of the professional staff and were excited to see how touched and blessed they were.

We gave the director some money and prayed for the administrative staff. It was wonderful to see the staff emotionally touched by our prayers. Papa Stanciu, one of our host fathers, was very moved by this orphanage and their need for sheets, pillowcases, and bed covers. Papa suggested that if our team paid for the cost of material, he would have his daughters sew all the necessary sheets, pillowcases, and bed covers the orphanage needed. We told Papa that we would buy the material. The director was very excited and so was Papa Stanciu. We prayed and blessed the director one last time before we left. Every time we blessed someone, we saw the power of our prayers being answered. This entire experience is far beyond my ability to write or describe. It was nothing short of miraculous.

Then Kathleen called and she was very excited. The little boy we had prayed for with the brain damage and headaches was completely healed and she said he had run to her and wrapped himself around her and wouldn't let go. The mother who had lost her little girl, Emma, in the car accident, was filled with the Holy Spirit and told Kathleen that she just wanted to be a servant of Jesus. At the previous night's Bible study, 22 wanted to be preachers, evangelists, and/or servants of God. Both of the girls who had severe toothaches were much better and were going to the dentist again for another treatment. The pastor there used some of the cash we gave him to fix the leaky roof for a family. Kathleen said they were able to buy two water heaters for the two apartments that did not have water heaters. The girls were very happy and their spirits were uplifted, thanks to our prayers and the gifts. Kathleen also thanked us for praying for her as she received peace and freedom from our prayers. Doubt and fear had impacted her and our prayers blessed her significantly. I told Kathleen that she would be receiving several boxes of food from the container shipment. We were all very excited about what God had done.

We headed over to the church to meet and worship on our last day in Romania. Worship was awesome. One of our host families' mothers came forward to receive prayer. Her name was Valle and she was doubled over in back pain and had been miserable for days. I suspected that she was carrying a backpack of burdens: perfection (trying to be perfect instead of trusting in Jesus' perfection); judgment (believing her pain was God's judgment on her); fear of paralysis and crippling disease (fear that no one would take care of her children); condemnation (she condemned herself and felt that God condemned her, too); anxiety, worry, and stress.

We asked Jesus to take the backpack from her. Valle saw a vision of Jesus taking the burdens off of her back, and of herself stepping out of a prison cell. She was set free.

Next we prayed for a woman with the fear of cancer. She also had a spirit of judgment and condemnation. But, there is no condemnation for those who are in Christ. Jesus takes all of your judgment from you. After praying for her, her face was filled with joy and hope.

As we went outside the church, Valle came running toward me from across the street. She was jumping up and down and screaming and praising God! She ran up to me and jumped in my arms. What a joy she felt and no back pain! Her back was completely healed. I have never seen anyone happier than Valle at that moment! Her enthusiasm and joy were amazing! It was also very contagious! Thank you Jesus for Valle. She told us that everything we prayed for was true and that she was set free!

I got on the airplane after saying a difficult goodbye to all of our new friends and suddenly felt much lighter. The air was clean and I began to reflect on all of the amazing miracles that we had witnessed. Thank you Lord for this wonderful trip! We all prayed for the Lord's continued blessing for the beautiful children and people of Romania. We will miss them.

"There is therefore now no condemnation for those who are in Christ Jesus. For the law of the Spirit of life in Christ Jesus has set you free from the law of sin and death."

Romans 8:1-2 (NKJV)

The Lord redeems us from death and condemnation. His resurrection is our resurrection.

Douglas F. Wall

REDEMPTION

CHAPTER 16

THIS IS
BUSINESS

Ever since I was in grade school, I had thought about starting and building my own business. I didn't know what I wanted to do, but I knew that someday I would run my own company. Both of my grandfathers had had their own businesses. My dad had his own business. There was something in me that just wanted to experience the excitement and the freedom of launching and growing a thriving enterprise. My mom taught me how to play chess at a very early age, and I enjoyed the strategic elements of the game, including having to anticipate several moves ahead. As a child, I excelled in math and I loved solving mathematical equations and number problems. Mind and logic problems and puzzles intrigued me enough that I used to purchase math puzzles, problem-solving books, and other mind-challenging games.

Business is very similar to playing chess or solving a puzzle. You need to be able to think strategically and consider future moves as well as anticipate obstacles and challenges in order to mitigate risks.

During my second year of college, I took an accounting class and it reminded me of solving math puzzles. After that class, I decided to become a business major with an emphasis in accounting. I graduated from San Diego State University in 1980, interviewed with the "big eight" accounting firms, and decided to accept a position with the San Diego office of Arthur Andersen & Company because I really enjoyed the people. I spent three years with Arthur Andersen, working in their audit department serving clients that needed their financial statements audited. I wasn't a particularly gifted auditor, but I learned a great deal and made a lot of friends. My career with Arthur Andersen ended after three years when the managing partner called me into his office and told me it was time for me to start looking for a new company. He was counseling me out of the firm. I wasn't completely surprised by this move, but I knew it was time for me to make a change. My heart and passion were not in being an auditor. Nevertheless, I was grateful for my time at Arthur Andersen.

In the fall of 1983, I joined Ernst & Whinney's Privately Owned Emerging Business department (POEB). It was here at Ernst that I really grew professionally, and from 1983 to 1985 I was assigned numerous small business clients to serve in various areas including tax, accounting, and consulting. In the five years that I spent in public accounting with Arthur Andersen and Ernst & Whinney, I went through five different managing partners and realized that not one of those managing partners was a true owner with freedom. They were simply employees of very large, bureaucratic, process-driven organizations. I also came to understand that not one of those managing partners was particularly happy in his job. It was simply a job and not a passion.

While I was at Ernst, in the summer of 1985, I received a letter from the CEO of a medical device and safety products manufacturing firm, who was a client of mine. The letter asked me if I could refer to him a part-time Chief Financial Officer (CFO) or controller. I remember reading the letter and thinking to myself, what a brilliant idea, a part-time CFO. Most small companies can't afford a full-time CFO but they do need that level of professional expertise.

The same year, my friend John started a part-time CFO/Controller company. I referred John to my client and suddenly we both had the same client. I started working directly with John who was now a contracted CFO/controller for my client. John and I met several times during 1985 to discuss our mutual client and, as he shared with me his passion and enthusiasm for the work he was doing, it occurred to me that this was what I wanted to do and what I was supposed to do. Instead of being an employee of a large organization, I wanted to contract with several clients, providing accounting, tax, consulting, and other financial advice to growth companies. In the fall of 1985, with much prayer and excitement, I decided it was time for me to join with John and form a new company, Resource Consulting Group, Inc. (RCG Management).

I look back on that decision, and realize that it was a huge act of faith to leave the employ of a very financially strong and reputable company to start a new business. The Lord is truly with us when we take bold steps in faith and in His will and timing. When I gave notice to the managing partner of Ernst & Whinney's San Diego office in December 1985, he referred me to my very first client, a dental services network, which turned out to require two days per week of my time. Amazingly, I made more in two days per week than on a full-time salary at Ernst & Whinney. This client gave me more than enough time to build and grow our new business. I was thrilled!

Both of these initial clients later became very successful enterprises. Our company RCG Management started off on solid ground. Being the owner of a small business is a serious test of faith and endurance. I had to wear many hats as a small business owner. Our small company became a solution for CEOs to be able to outsource key aspects of the management of their company. We expanded from financial services to human resources, sales, marketing, information systems and other services. We even offered contracted Chief Executive Officer (CEO) services. As part of our compensation, we requested to be paid in both cash and equity. Equity was given to us in the form of stock options, warrants, or sometimes founders' shares.

Over the next 16 years, our Company served over 2,000 emerging growth companies. We provided management services to every type and stage of company, ranging from startups to Fortune 1,000 companies. Our payroll grew from two people to over 100 employees. When you are serving that many small businesses, you get an opportunity to see a lot of unique and very interesting things.

For example, there was the time we had just engaged with a new client and he told us that he had three sets of accounting books. The first set of records for the IRS showed that the business had losses. The second set of books for his bank showed that the business made profits. The third set of books for himself revealed what was actually happening. We counseled our client to have only one set of accounting records to simplify his life and to help him focus on building the business, instead of wasting valuable time, energy, and resources on questionable and untruthful bookkeeping and accounting. This is one example of hundreds of unique situations we had to address.

Because RCG's clients were typically referred by our clients' CPA firm, bank, or law firm, we often were forced to confront the President, CEO, or the Board on critical issues including: improper business practices, employee and management criminal activity, tax evasion and fraud, sexual harassment, control and intimidation tactics, and numerous other inappropriate or immoral business decisions or practices. RCG became a highly trusted advisor to its clients' executive teams. Working with emerging growth companies is a tremendous challenge because you are constantly dealing with crises and resolving conflicts. Entrepreneurs seem to attract crises and conflicts. Our firm gained deep expertise and acquired a highly successful track record of solving problems for growth companies. It was now making sense why I used to spend so much time as a kid solving riddles, math problems, and puzzles. The Lord was preparing me to help solve real-life problems.

The truth is God is the solver of business problems. In the early stages of our company's growth, we decided to take on a third partner. This particular partner was given a salary and specific objectives. He was supposed to invest a large sum to cover his salary for one year. At the end of six months, none of those objectives was accomplished and although he had committed to invest, he withdrew his commitment. Over those six months, we had paid him a large salary plus benefits and none of his time was billable to clients. I remember clearly the day John and I met to try to solve the problem of being $100,000 in debt as a direct result of our decision to take on this partner. It was the first time we had prayed together. That day, we turned our business over to the Lord and from that point on, amazing things started happening. For me, it was an extremely valuable lesson, and we became a lot more diligent with regard to taking on equity investors/partners.

When you are working with cash-strapped, emerging companies as clients, making payroll is always a challenge. We had to make 24 payrolls each year for 16 years and, amazingly, we were able to make every one. There were dozens and dozens of times we were able to pick up a check or two from clients on or just before the day payroll was due. We affectionately called this "just-in-time funding." This was the Lord's interesting way of developing our trust in Him. To this day, I am still completely amazed at how the Lord continually blessed our clients with "just-in-time funding." We found out that faith in God and the power of prayer is critical in business.

One of my dearest mentors and friends was a man named Bill. Bill was a highly regarded and successful entrepreneur who decided to give back to entrepreneurs. In 1985, Bill founded a non-profit organization called UCSD Connect. The purpose of Connect was to partner with the University of California, San Diego, and assist entrepreneurs by connecting them to both capital providers and service providers. Capital providers included banks, venture capital funds, and high net worth individual investors, which the business community calls "Angels." Service providers included attorneys, accountants, and various consultants like RCG.

I watched Bill become one of the most connected people in San Diego just by connecting people. The Lord gave me the idea to be an example and model our firm after Connect by coming alongside entrepreneurs and surrounding them with key introductions that we thought could be helpful. For the next decade, RCG became a magnet for entrepreneurs looking for capital and help in growing their business. We never seemed to have a shortage of emerging companies looking for help. Sometimes we even got paid for this help.

In 1992, RCG started organizing CEO Roundtables. We invited 10 to 15 CEOs to participate in a two-hour "virtual board" session focused on a particular topic. The topics ranged from raising capital, developing a sales and marketing plan, and protecting intellectual property, to hiring a key executive. Over the next nine years, RCG organized over 300 unique roundtables and developed strong relationships with hundreds of CEOs. More importantly, the Lord gave us favor and grace as we gained invaluable insight and wisdom by listening to the experiences and advice from many seasoned CEOs. The roundtable format also became the genesis of several viable businesses including two private equity venture capital funds, a couple of industry councils, and an angel investing group, all of which are continuing to provide assistance and support to emerging companies today.

In 1999, we made the decision to raise a venture capital round of financing and to expand nationally. We believed we had built something very unique in San Diego. Our goal was to build a global organization that would serve small- to medium-sized growth companies. We also made a strategic decision to build a very unique "Software as a Service Platform" that would enable CEOs to strategically manage their business via a digital dashboard, revealing the critical back office areas of their company including: financial and accounting, human resources, sales and marketing, and IT. Additionally, we populated the platform with over 1,000 knowledge objects. We changed the name of the company from RCG to Alitum and raised over $11 million in venture capital investment. In 2001, Alitum grew to over 100 employees with $10 million in revenues. We signed up several private equity venture capital firms and their portfolio companies as clients. We were on our way to expand nationally and internationally.

September 11th changed everything. During the month of September 2001, I was in Romania on a mission trip when I found out that our board of directors had decided to pull the plug on our company. They called it an orderly wind down. I came home on October 5th and the company that I had co-founded, grown, and nurtured for 16 years was suddenly no longer in existence. I could not understand why the venture capital firm that now had a controlling interest in my company had decided to shut it down and why they could not have waited a couple of weeks until I returned so we could at least have had a board meeting to discuss our options. I guess I will never know. I do know that there are quite a few things I don't understand and that short of the grave, I just will not know. One thing I do know is that God was preparing me for greater things. My time with RCG and Alitum was not in vain. God is in control.

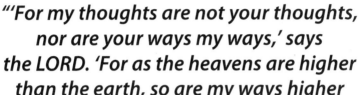

*"'For my thoughts are not your thoughts,
nor are your ways my ways,' says
the LORD. 'For as the heavens are higher
than the earth, so are my ways higher
than your ways, and my thoughts
than your thoughts.'"*

Isaiah 55:6-9 (NKJV)

*The Lord redeems business failures,
bankruptcy, poverty,
and financial disasters.*

Douglas F. Wall

REDEMPTION

CHAPTER 17

DONNA'S REDEMPTION

My sister Donna died in 1959 when I was only 18 months old. Growing up, my parents did not talk about Donna's death very much as it was a very traumatic and painful event in their lives. My father, mother, brother, and two sisters were a close family, but there was an underlying sadness in our home. Donna was five months old when she died of crib death. It is a very interesting coincidence that her death was so similar to my daughter Courtney's death. Donna

111

was my parents' third child and was born in 1958; Courtney was Therese's and my third child who was born in 1988. Donna lived for five months and Courtney lived for three months.

In a scientific paper published October 29, 2008 in the *Journal of Neuroscience,* Dr. Louise Faber states: "Our strongest and most vivid human memories are usually associated with strong emotional events such as those associated with extreme fear, love and rage. For many of us, our deepest memories are mental snapshots taken during times of high emotional impact or involvement."

By 2004, I had received prayer for healing over Courtney's death, but no one had ever prayed for me specifically for Donna's death. I simply did not know or believe that I needed prayer for that particular day in my life, mainly because I believed I was just too young to remember. The truth is our brains are more powerful than computers and can store vast amounts of information that trigger memories through our senses, such as with a song, a sight, a touch, taste, or even smell. They say during brain surgery we can also remember long-forgotten experiences. All I can say from my personal experience is that the Holy Spirit can perform very precise surgery with much more accuracy and much more powerful healing.

A major turning point for me in dealing with Courtney's death was the day I asked the Lord to redeem my relationship with my father. Normally, when I got together with my dad, we would have small talk about family, work, sports, or the weather, but not about anything meaningful.

That day the Lord put one question in my heart to ask my dad: "Was it difficult for you to bury one of your children?"

As I asked the question, I will never forget my dad's eyes riveted on mine, both of us staring at each other, waiting for an answer.

Our eyes filled with tears and, his voice straining and cracking, my dad answered:

"Yes it was hard, but not nearly as hard as seeing you go through the same thing."

I was 35 years old and that was the very first day I had a meaningful talk with my dad. We cried together, we laughed together, and for the first time in my life, I had a real relationship with my father. We even hugged and told each other that we loved each other. From this point on, I knew I would never be the same.

I had seen God redeem Courtney's death through prayer and also through the cathartic conversation with my dad. So, at a prayer meeting in 2004 when Sharon, one of my close friends who is usually very quiet, indicated that she felt strongly that the group should pray for me specifically for my sister's death, I willingly participated. Immediately, I could feel my face flush and I could sense that the Lord was going to lead this prayer time. Sharon, my wife, and my friends gathered around me and asked the Lord to heal the wounds from the death of my sister. As I closed my eyes, the Holy Spirit took me back to the memory of the day in 1958 that Donna died.

It's a strange thing to go back into a memory that has been buried for 46 years. The first thing I recall was the total shock on my parents' faces. Their expressions contained a whole host of intense emotions including panic, horror, terror, fear, helplessness, and intense sadness. As I vividly recalled my parent's faces, I started to remember and feel everything that was happening that day and the painful emotions were overwhelming. The intense pain felt like a knife in my stomach and I doubled over in agony, groaning with indescribable pain.

There was part of me that did not want to remember. I just wanted to quit and forget the whole thing. My daughter Courtney's death was painful but this was even more intense by a factor of ten. I sensed that the Lord wanted to heal me and I made a conscience decision to keep going. I was experiencing intense fear remembering how frightened and alone I had felt at the time. I felt like the walls of our home were caving in around me like a suffocating darkness.

As my friends prayed, they asked the Lord to reveal to me all the untruths and lies associated with this memory. I was shaking uncontrollably as the lies came pouring forth like a flood:

Death has authority over my dad and mom. I am alone and abandoned. I am condemned to death. I am panicked, dreadful and hopeless. Death is powerful and it is in control. Death has complete control of my parents and my home. I see the look of intense fright–I no longer have peace and comfort.

I am ruled by death. Death has authority of our home. Death's power is profound. I am disconnected. I am isolated and all alone. I am discarded and sentenced to death. Death is in charge; death is in control. Death is in authority over all. My emotions are dead. My passions, hopes, confidence and trust are dead.

Death has come and now takes residence in my home. Death has full authority to reign. Death has power to control my thoughts and my actions. Death rules. I am terrified, lost, lonely, frightened, terrorized, deeply troubled, helpless, hopeless, and distressed. I am in the dark. I am discarded and left to die. I am the next in line to die. There is no one to rescue me. There is nowhere to hide. This is it. There is Nothing.

What is the point of living? I hate life. I hate myself. I am better dead than alive.

Death is consuming—all consuming. Death has poured itself into me and into the core of who I am. Death impacts everything. Not one thing is spared from death. Darkness is in control. I am shaken. I am trembling knowing that I will never be the same. Death is my life. Death is my death. Death is my creator. Death is my God. Death is all I have. I am nothing. I am worthless. I am meaningless. I am insignificant. I am thrown away to the pit of Hell. Nothing. Empty.

As my friends continued to pray, they asked the Lord to take authority over the lies and reveal the truth: "And you shall know the truth, and the truth shall make you free" (John 8:32, NKJV).

Here is what the Holy Spirit showed me during this prayer time:

I am immediately taken into heaven. I am with the Lord and we are together in a mansion inside. The mansion has a huge front door with an amazing overhanging roof over the circular driveway.

Next, I see several black-hooded death riders like angels of death on black horses coming to the front door. There appear to be nine of them and they look like the black-hooded death riders from the "Lord of the Rings" movie. The lead rider is Death with Murder, Suicide, Horror, Panic, Terror, Fear, Anxiety, and Despair close behind. The death riders have come to take me away from my home. They are leading me to death.

I see the Lord stand up and I am speechless as I see Him walk up to the front door.

He opens the door and reveals His blood on the top and sides of the front door posts.

I now see the hooded, black death riders ride away and pass over my home and I am reminded of the amazing Passover story in the book of Exodus.

Right then, I realized that Jesus has authority over all. Jesus has authority of my life, my home, and my soul. Jesus is with me forever. I am not alone. Jesus is my Savior, King and High Priest in heaven, my Lord, and my God. Death is not in control and does not have me. I am secure in Christ. Jesus is my salvation. Jesus is the creator of all things. The entire universe was created by Him. Jesus has authority over all that he creates. Jesus has authority over death.

My home is secure. It is marked by the blood of Christ. My Lord will always be with me. He will never leave me. He says: "I am your God. Trust me. My blood covers your front door. You are pardoned. I have sent death away. You are mine. You are my special son. I receive you from the stronghold of death. You are free. Nothing can separate you from me now. Nothing. Not even death. Death no longer shall have dominion in your home. Your home is safe. It is a refuge. I dwell in your home; your home is My home and My home is your home. I am your Father.

"I am your stronghold and your shield. Come to Me and I will show you the mysteries of heaven and earth. Where your treasure lies–look for Me. I will show you treasure: hidden treasure. Do not seek after wealth. Seek first the Kingdom of God and all these things will follow. I am your Father. I am your friend. Trust in Me."

"And the blood shall be to you for a token upon the houses where ye are: and when I see the blood, I will pass over you, and the plague shall not be upon you to destroy you."

Exodus 12:13 (NKJV)

"But when this corruptible shall put on incorruption, and when this mortal shall put on immortality, then will take place the word that is written, Death is swallowed up in victory. O death, where is your sting? O grave, where is your victory? The sting of death is sin, and the strength of sin is the law. But thanks be to God who gives us the victory through our Lord Jesus Christ."

1 Corinthians 15: 54-57 (NKJV)

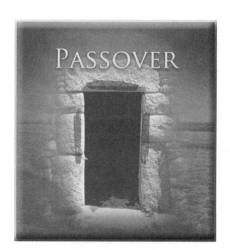

The Lord redeems us from death unto life.

Douglas F. Wall

CHAPTER 18

POWER OF PRAYER

In 1997, I invested $20,000 in a start-up Internet company. In 1999, I received a call from one of the board members of this company telling me that the $20k investment was now worth over $200k as the result of a merger with a public company. Over the next few months, the public company's stock skyrocketed, increasing the value of my shares from an initial $20k investment to nearly $4 million. In the venture capital world, this investment return is considered a home run and would provide the means to return the total fund back to the investors. In the gambling world, this would be the equivalent of hitting the jackpot or winning the lottery. The odds of being blessed with a 200x return on investment are so high that I knew it was clearly a gift from God.

In 2000, the Lord inspired me with scriptures that encouraged me to reinvest the $4 million.

"Lay not up for yourselves treasures upon earth where moth and rust doth corrupt, and where thieves break through and steal. But lay up for yourselves treasures in heaven, where neither moth nor rust doth

corrupt, and where thieves to not break through nor steal: For where your treasure is, there will your heart be also" (Matthew 6:19-21, NKJV).

"And he spake a parable unto them, saying, The ground of a certain rich man brought forth plentifully: And he thought within himself, saying, What shall I do, because I have no room where to bestow my fruits? And he said, This will I do: I will pull down my barns, and build greater; and there will I bestow all my fruits and my goods. And I will say to my soul, Soul, thou hast much goods laid up for many years; take thine ease, eat, drink and be merry. But God said unto him, Thou fool, this night thy soul shall be required of thee: then whose shall those things be, which thou hast provided? So is he that layeth up treasure for himself, and is not rich towards God" (Luke 12:16-21, NKJV).

"For the kingdom of heaven is like a man traveling to a far country, who called his own servants and delivered his goods to them. And to one he gave five talents, to another two, and to another one, to each according to his own ability; and immediately he went on a journey. Then he who had received the five talents went and traded with them, and made another five talents.

"And likewise he who had received two gained two more also. But he who had received one went and dug in the ground, and hid his lord's money. After a long time the lord of those servants came and settled accounts with them. "So he who had received five talents came and brought five other talents, saying, 'Lord, you delivered to me five talents; look, I have gained five more talents besides them.'

"His lord said to him, 'Well done, good and faithful servant; you were faithful over a few things, I will make you ruler over many things. Enter into the joy of your lord.' He also who had received two talents came and said, 'Lord, you delivered to me two talents; look, I have gained two more talents besides them.'

"His lord said to him, 'Well done, good and faithful servant; you have been faithful over a few things, I will make you ruler over many things. Enter into the joy of your lord.'

"Then he who had received the one talent came and said, 'Lord, I knew you to be a hard man, reaping where you have not sown, and gathering where you have not scattered seed. And I was afraid, and went and hid your talent in the ground. Look, there you have what is yours.'

"But his lord answered and said to him, 'You wicked and lazy servant, you knew that I reap where I have not sown, and gather where I have not scattered seed. So you ought to have deposited my money with the bankers, and at my coming I would have received back my own with interest.

"Therefore take the talent from him, and give it to him who has ten talents. 'For to everyone who has, more will be given, and he will have abundance; but from him who does not have, even what he has will be taken away. And cast the unprofitable servant into the outer darkness. There will be weeping and gnashing of teeth. '" (Matthew 25:14-30, NKJV).

By the end of 2004, the entire $4 million and then some had been reinvested into dozens of start-up and growth companies, Kingdom enterprises, charitable organizations and other projects. I continued to hope for a large financial harvest that did not come. I was considering filing for personal bankruptcy when I met a man by the name of Bruce Cook. We were introduced by a mutual friend on the telephone during a business call. Bruce prayed over me words of life about my circumstances, my family, my identity and destiny, and immediately I realized that the Lord was going to take me to a new level of trust and build a more solid foundation of faith in me.

What Bruce spoke over me were not just empty words, but God's power to activate inside of me faith and peace to trust God. Over the course of the next several months, the Lord delivered me from the bondage of debt and money anxiety, and I was able to forgive several people who had wronged me in business. This time in my life was nothing short of a miracle and became a turning point which opened the door to a new season with new opportunities and relationships. I could feel life returning to me, and hope growing inside of me about my future. My wife and family could also see the difference. I witnessed firsthand the miracle of God in small and sometimes large, practical ways by learning how to trust in our provider, Jehovah Jireh.

"Therefore, if anyone is in Christ, he is a new creation; the old has gone, the new has come!"

2 Corinthians 5:17 (NKJV)

"And when you stand praying, if you hold anything against anyone, forgive him, so that your Father in heaven may forgive you your sins. "

Mark 11:25 (NKJV)

The Lord redeems us from our fears, anxieties and worries including poverty, bankruptcy and financial failure.

Douglas F. Wall

REDEMPTION

CHAPTER 19

LET THERE
BE LIGHT

In 2002, I was in the process of forming a new company whose mission would be to come alongside entrepreneurs and early stage companies and provide help, encouragement and support with the business plan, growth capital, management and strategic direction. Previously, I had come across the Greek word "Kairos," which means God's time. After purchasing a Greek-English and English-Greek dictionary, I looked up the word "time" and discovered the word "Genea," which means Genesis.

I believe the name Genea is awesome because it honors God our Creator. Genesis, the first book of the Bible, wonderfully describes the miracle of creation and Genea means beginning of time, formation, creating life from void, fullness from emptiness, and light from darkness.

"In the beginning God created the heavens and the earth. And the earth was without form and empty. And darkness was on the face of the deep. And the Spirit of God moved on the face of the waters. And God said, Let there be light and there was light. And God saw the light that it was good. And God divided between the light and the darkness. And God called the light, Day. And He called the darkness, Night. And the evening and the morning were the first day" (Genesis 1:1-5, NKJV).

Genea Advisors worked with and helped a number of unique technology and software companies. It was an amazing time for me and I clearly saw the hand of God as well as His redeeming power. The single most important ingredient of Genea's success was that Bruce Cook, led by the Holy Spirit, inspired me to form an intercessory prayer team to pray specifically for Genea. Bruce and I give full glory to God as He has been our inspiration for accomplishing much more than we ever expected, including:

- Development of comprehensive business plans and strategic revenue models

- Recruitment of Management Teams and Board of Directors

- Raising over $20 million in private equity

- Issuance of numerous patents and trademarks and the development of an enforceable intellectual property portfolio

- Signed contracts with global customers

- Recognition in National media and publications

Each new company I meet is clearly a divine appointment. I trust in the Lord who redeems us in more ways that we will ever know.

"Do not be conformed to this world, but be transformed by the renewal of your mind, that by testing you may discern what is the will of God, what is good and acceptable and perfect."

Romans 12:2 (NKJV)

"And he has filled him with the Spirit of God, with skill, with intelligence, with knowledge, and with all craftsmanship, to devise artistic designs, to work in gold and silver and bronze."

Exodus 35:31-32 (NKJV)

The Lord redeems us from the mediocre traditional and conventional and brings forth extraordinary creativity and innovation.

Douglas F. Wall

CHAPTER 20

PUREFORGE®

I met Nathan Meckel in 1994 and from that moment on I knew we would become close friends. There are a handful of people you meet in life that you connect with immediately. Nathan had just started a company that focused on extending the service life of knife blades and other cutting surfaces. Unlike the vast majority of scientists, technologists, and inventors, Nathan was quite engaging, personable, and humble. From 1994 to 2006, our friendship continued to grow as we worked closely together. I was amazed at Nathan's ability to stay optimistic in the face of trials and adversity. I was also blessed by his willingness to receive counsel and direction.

In 2006, we co-founded the company, Tech M3, Inc., initially working on extending the service life of brake systems. It seemed ludicrous to think that anyone could develop a brake rotor that does not wear and would outlast the life of the vehicle. Everything in life wears down, corrodes, decays, rusts, gets destroyed, and eventually disintegrates and dies. Nothing seems to last anymore. We have developed a disposable lifestyle in the modern age.

Initially, we focused our efforts on motorcycle brake rotors. Our strategy was to develop an extremely wear-resistant brake rotor and pad that were also better performing. Since 2006, our understanding of the science behind brake friction has grown exponentially. We continue to make new discoveries and exciting advancements in brake systems, and have expanded to the point of offering brake solutions to government and commercial fleets.

The genius of inventing something new and remarkable is truly a miracle. We are quite astonished when miracles happen and we stare in unbelief and say, 'What just happened?' Think about what it must have been like to be there at Kitty Hawk, N.C. the day the Wright brothers first took flight or the day Thomas Edison finally found the filament that would work for his light bulb! It must have been memorable as well as historic!

In 2010, I joined the company full time and we made the strategic decision to focus on providing Brakes as a Service® to law enforcement and commercial fleets. We needed to develop a brand name that would be appropriate for the company. One day I was driving from San Diego to Los Angeles with my 14-year-old daughter, Elise, to pick up my wife at the LAX airport. Nathan was in his vehicle behind me. Our goal was to meet in Orange County with a branding company to discuss the development of a new brand name and after the meeting, Elise and I would continue on to the airport and Nathan would head back to San Diego. My daughter asked me, "Dad, why do we have to stop for a business meeting?" I told her that Nathan and I were trying to develop a new name for our company. Elise asked me what our company does and I explained that we have developed Atomic-Forged® technology that eliminates wear in brakes, makes them much safer and eliminates toxic brake dust and brake fade. She thought about what I said for a moment, and then said, "How about PureForge®?"

As soon as she said PureForge®, I knew that this name was from God. I immediately called Nathan and was so excited that the Lord had given us an amazing new name, out of the mouths of babes!

Everything about PureForge® has been an incredible gift from God. Not only do PureForge® brakes significantly improve safety and performance by eliminating brake fade, warping, corrosion, squeaking and providing shorter stopping distances, they also drastically eliminate the toxic hazards of brake dust, and at the same time offer a cost savings. As PureForge® expands , Nathan and I are confident in the Lord's direction. Similar to Genea, the single most important ingredient of PureForge®'s success has been the formation of an intercessory prayer team to pray for the Company's management, employees, customers, partners, investors, vendors, suppliers, manufacturers, distributors, and especially for those who are driving vehicles equipped with PureForge® brakes. The PureForge® team gives full glory to God as He has been our inspiration for accomplishing much more than we could have ever imagined.

In June of 2012, Reo Carr, the editor for the *San Diego Business Journal,* came to visit PureForge. We gave him a tour of our headquarters and then allowed him to test drive our police car equipped with PureForge® brakes. Reo gave the brakes a good run for the money and came back to our manufacturing facilities and he was pretty excited about how well the PureForge® brakes had performed. He was also very enthusiastic about the PureForge® story and told Nathan and I that he would like to put the PureForge® story on the front page of the *San Diego Business Journal* and that the headline would say: "WE BRAKE FOR MONEY." I looked over at Nathan and he looked back at me and we did not say anything to Reo about the choice of the headline. Instead, I went home that night and prayed and on Saturday morning I continued to ask God for a better headline for the story. I told the Lord, "I'll take anything but 'We brake for money,'" and I started thinking, "What about 'We brake for health,' or 'We brake for safety,'" and then it came to me:

"WE BRAKE FOR LIFE."®

I knew that this was a download from heaven! I emailed Nathan and he loved it and I couldn't wait to call Reo on Monday morning and tell him.

On Monday morning, an email was sent to both Nathan and I from one of the Police Officers who had been riding a motorcycle with our brakes for approximately two weeks. The email is as follows:

"PureForge® brakes saved two lives this week, mine and an elderly gentleman's. The gentleman crossed the road about 100 yards in front of me. He suddenly fell backward in front of me. I immediately applied maximum braking and came to a complete stop about six inches from his head. Fortunately, no one was hurt. I am very grateful to God that I was able to react appropriately and avoid hitting him. I'm also very grateful for my PureForge® brakes that seemed to 'Stop on a dime' when I needed them most."

—Officer Michael Garcia
City of Escondido, California Motor Officer

When Nathan and I read this email, we both shed a tear, realizing that the Lord had given us quite a prophetic word. I then forwarded the email to Reo, along with the new slogan God had just given us for the company. To our surprise and delight, he used that as his headline for the article. "We Brake for Life®" has multiple meanings, including:

- We brake for the life the of the vehicle as our brake rotors will outlast the life of the vehicle.
- We brake for the life of the environment which includes plant, animal and human lives.
- We brake for the life of the people driving our brakes as our brakes stop shorter.
- We brake for the life of others such as pedestrians as well.

But, the most single most important meaning behind "We Brake for Life®" is:

- Jesus is the way, the truth and the life. We brake for Jesus!

PureForge's Atomic-Forged® brake rotors were recognized as the most significant mechanical design innovation of 2013 by R&D Magazine. The prestigious and influential R&D 100 awards are considered the "Oscars of Innovation" and recognize the top 100 technology innovations of the year. As the *Wall Street Journal* quoted Nathan Meckel, co-founder and Chief Technology Officer, "We are not inventors; we are discoverers of God's inventions."

PureForge® has become the leading innovator in the brake industry and has developed an extensive intellectual property portfolio of issued patents and a significant pipeline of pending patents, trademarks and copyrights. The PureForge® team is extremely grateful to the members of Mintz Levin, our law firm which has been at the forefront of PureForge®'s intellectual property protection strategy as well as assisting us in the execution phase of our licensing strategic growth plan.

Two close friends of mine, Kevin and Jackie Freiberg, are the authors of *Nuts* and *Nanovation* and say there is a huge and growing movement centered around innovation. "We believe innovation is the lifeblood of job creation, cleaning up the environment and producing products that not only save lives but they promote new life," said the Freibergs.

One of the passions of the PureForge® team is to encourage young people to become innovators and entrepreneurs. It is our dream to create, inspire, and fund entrepreneurial innovations for middle school, junior high, high school, and college students. We believe there are many exciting and creative ways to inspire our young entrepreneurs, including: competitions, awards, scholarships, internships, collaboration and mentoring in the areas of Innovation, Science, Mathematics, Business Plans, Engineering, Graphic Arts, and Performing Arts.

I believe that one must also have a *personal* vision/mission statement in order to move from success to significance. In May 2000, I created mine:

- Be a shining light to those in darkness
- Transform innovations, ideas, and visions into thriving enterprises that give glory to God

- Connect people together—match needs with resources
- Help others achieve personal freedom by pointing them to Jesus, the way, the truth, and the life
- Encourage, empower, and love people with the heavenly Father's love
- Speak courageously and passionately to people about Christ who gives us life, hope, and faith
- Give away grace and favor and share the gifts, talents, and enthusiasm God has given me
- Listen to God, ask for wisdom, and give generously as the Lord has given generously to me
- Rejoice evermore, give thanks in all things, and pray without ceasing
- Give Jesus all the glory, praise, and thanks
- Forgive freely just as Jesus has forgiven me

My spirit soars as a result of knowing with certainty and clarity why I have been created! That is because I believe God gave me a purpose, a special purpose—His purpose.

The Lord calls all of us to a big life. There is no better feeling in the world than to work on something you totally believe in and know in your heart of hearts that what you are doing is helping people. I am so thankful to God that He has not only blessed me with meaning and purpose but also that I have been given the opportunity to make a significant impact in this world. I believe there is no greater purpose than to serve God's purpose.

"If you keep yourself pure, you will be a utensil God can use for his purpose. Your life will be clean, and you will be ready for the Master to use you for every good work."

2 Timothy 2:21 (NKJV)

"But I have raised you up for this very purpose, that I might show you My power and that my name might be proclaimed in all the earth."

Exodus 9:16 (NKJV)

"For it is God who works in you to will and to act according to His good purpose."

Philippians 2:13 (NKJV)

The Lord redeems His purpose in us including His creativity and innovation.

Douglas F. Wall

CHAPTER 21

FREEDOM

One of my all-time favorite movies is *The Shawshank Redemption*. It and other prison-break movies, like *The Great Escape*, *The Count of Monte Cristo*, and *Cool Hand Luke*, celebrate the human spirit and its divinely-given passion to be free. I think I have watched *Shawshank* at least two dozen times. If I had a better memory, I would have all the lines memorized by now. It is set in the 1940's when Andy Dufresne, played by Tim Robbins, is sent to Shawshank Prison for the murder of his wife and lover. Andy is very isolated and lonely at first, but comes to realize that there is something deep inside of us that nothing—no one, not prison guards, or even prison walls—can take away: hope. Andy becomes friends with

Red, played by Morgan Freeman, and shows Red why it is crucial to have hope and the dream of freedom. Fear can hold each of us prisoner. Hope can set us free.

Shawshank does an amazing job of revealing what the average person struggles with—the fear and immobilization that can set in when our freedoms are threatened. I'm not talking about the chafing that comes from not getting to do what we want to do when we want to do it. Instead, I'm referring to the paralyzing sense that we have lost control of our most basic freedoms—among others, the freedom from worry, the freedom from habits that enslave us, and the freedom to be our best selves.

After graduating from San Diego State University, I started working for a large accounting firm. Working in a large bureaucratic company is like a prison sentence for an entrepreneur. Entrepreneurs don't like to follow a long list of rules, processes, and procedures. I am not a very good rule follower. Whether it was embarrassing my boss with a singing telegram on Saint Patrick's Day or playing practical jokes on my staff, I am wired to be free, to have fun when I work, when I worship, and when I play.

I don't want to suggest that entrepreneurs feel the loss of freedom more than others, but just to add the work environment to the list of the many situations in which I have felt confined. If you really think about it, it's easy to see that many of us are confined behind prison walls that are constructed of much more than brick and mortar. Anything that restrains, restricts, or limits our choices can feel like a prison wall. Whatever controls, dominates, or dehumanizes us becomes our prison.

But, some of these walls are of our own making, and they represent behaviors that harm us and others. In actual fact, I have created plenty of my own prisons over the years via unforgiveness, lies, and judgment. There are forces, thoughts, old patterns, and sins that keep us in bondage and keep us from experiencing freedom. And, if we see no way out, we are in danger of losing our hope.

Some time ago, a friend of mine asked to borrow money from me. I ended up borrowing money myself in order to lend to him. He promised to repay me and when he didn't, not only was I angry at him for breaking his promise, but I was angry at myself for doing something so foolish, despite my pure motivations. It didn't take long for my anger to turn to judgment and eventually bitterness.

I knew it was important to forgive my friend but the debt was significant and I could not let it go. I understood the power of being in bondage to monetary debt, and I was learning about the uncomfortable debt of unforgiveness as well. I cried out to the Lord to help me. Every time I read the Bible, the Lord pointed me toward mercy and forgiveness. My head would say the words of forgiveness but my heart wouldn't go along. Instead, I felt that my anger was justified because it was his fault for talking me into going into debt! I felt very little freedom during that time of my life because, lurking in the background of every success, was a cloud of anger and hurt.

When my friend filed for bankruptcy, I was devastated. I also considered filing for bankruptcy but the Lord directed me to trust Him instead. I asked the Lord to help me forgive this man and also to set me free from debt, judgment, and unforgiveness.

Jesus addressed freedom when He was on the earth—once in the temple when He opened a prophecy from the Old Testament book of Isaiah and read, *"The spirit of the Sovereign Lord is on me because he has anointed me to preach good news to the poor. He has sent me to proclaim freedom for the prisoners and recovery of sight for the blind. To release the oppressed to proclaim the year of the Lord's favor."*

Another time Jesus said to Jewish believers in Jerusalem, *"If you hold to my teaching, you are really my disciples. Then you will know the truth and the truth will set you free. . . . So if the Son sets you free you will be free indeed."*

When I became a follower of Jesus, He set me free from all of my sins and debts. When I withheld forgiveness from my friend, I was placing myself back in bondage to new debts that I didn't want to release. Unforgiveness is a no-win proposition. Everyone gets damaged. The Lord spoke to me in His word: 'Withhold forgiveness and your forgiveness will be withheld. Do not hold onto the luggage of another man. Do not hold his sins or anyone's sins. Give forgiveness freely to others including yourself and God will show you His unlimited mercy and forgiveness. Mercy triumphs over judgment, and forgiveness has authority over the powers of darkness including sin and death.'

Over the next several years I was able to forgive my friend with my heart, not just my head, and trust the Lord to take away my judgment, anger and bitterness. As I forgave freely as Jesus forgives, I was able to be free. Finally, I was able to forgive myself and witness the Lord's mercy as He released me of all of my anger, judgment, unforgiveness and the condemnation I directed at myself.

As the Lord gave me a new attitude about my friend, He also changed my heart. Receiving the Lord's gift of forgiveness is an act of faith. I had to trust the Lord to redeem me. Thankfully, there will always be much more grace than there is sin.

Since then, my friend and I have grown very close. We love each other. We are brothers in Christ and He has become a trusted mentor as well as one of my dearest friends.

Freedom and redemption are joined at the hip. We all have a personal spirit and a heart, and all our spirits and hearts are wounded and broken to some degree and need healing, nurturing, and freeing. God gives each of us a purpose, a mission, but something tries to hold us back from fulfilling our mission. Jesus came to free us from that bondage. He does it by forgiving our sin, paying the price for our rebellion, healing us, and setting us free.

Hoping in the freedom that Jesus promises is vastly different than hoping in merely a good outcome of a sticky situation. Earthly hope is wishful thinking. Hope tied to Jesus and His promises is a sure thing.

I mentioned self-condemnation above. Despite the fact that I'm basically an optimistic, enthusiastic, positive person, I am well aware of my failings. My whole life I have pursued goals, ambitions, desires, and investments, desperately seeking comfort and happiness. Where did that desperation come from? Why was I feeling so insecure? Who knows? But, one night I woke up in the middle of the night thinking of all the things I needed to do the next day, how many things I still wanted to accomplish, and I grew overwhelmed at the implications of the list.

Every once in a while in life you get that "aha" moment. I keep a journal and try to write down my thoughts daily, and now and then the lights go on and I realize I finally understand something. That next morning God gave me an "aha" moment.

I have always known that God owns everything. God owns all the cattle on a thousand hills and He also owns all the diamonds in the world. He owns all the commercial real estate in New York as well as all the gold in Fort Knox. You would think that if I know that God owns everything and I trust God, then I would be happy and secure. The trouble is that for some reason, I was still seeking, pursuing, desiring, and looking for whatever would give me comfort and happiness, and remove my insecurity.

That morning God gave me a mental picture of what I call The Vault. He has given me keys to the vault. But, what is in it? The vault holds everything that I have ever wanted in life. Everything!

I asked the Lord again, "Do you mean everything?"

He said, "Yes. Everything."

So, I made a list of over 40 things representing everything I own, both tangible and intangible, including: security, love, access to people, wisdom, comfort, grace, persuasiveness, peace, solutions, effective prayer, joy, patience, mercy and compassion, hope, gentleness, forgiveness, discernment, freedom, creativity, wealth, healing, humility, generosity, heaven, travel, awesome memories, family, kindness, time, rest, trust, faith, respect, redemption, reputation, inheritance, destiny, identity, legacy, passion, confidence, boldness, courage, assurance, covenantal blessings and promises. And the list never ends.

And the key to the vault is Jesus! Jesus is the source of hope, forgiveness, healing, and freedom, and the giver of all these gifts.

"I find I'm so excited I can barely sit still or hold a thought in my head. I think it is the excitement only a free man can feel, a free man at the start of a long journey whose conclusion is uncertain. I hope I can make it across the border. I hope to see my friend, and shake his hand. I hope the Pacific is as blue as it has been in my dreams. I hope." Red Redding, *Shawshank Redemption*.

"Stand fast therefore in the freedom with which Christ has made us free and do not again be held with the yoke of bondage."

Galatians 5:1 (NKJV)

The Lord redeems our freedom

Douglas F. Wall

REDEMPTION

CHAPTER 22

WEDDING DAY —LET US REJOICE

My oldest child and daughter Melissa came to us in the spring of 2008 and told us she wanted to start socializing with a young man by the name of Nahum. I asked Melissa, "What kind of a name is Nahum?" She told me Nahum was actually a book in the Bible. I said, "It is? Where?" Sure enough, there it was, in the Old Testament between Micah and Habakkuk. The book of Nahum is one of those almost forgotten books in the Bible. It is only three pages long and is a follow up story to the book of Jonah. Nahum was a prophet of God who delivered several key lessons including God's jealousy, patience, mercy, and ultimately, judgment of Nineveh. We set up a time for Nahum to come to our home. This would be a perfect time for me to clean the guns.

As Therese, Nahum, Melissa and I all sat down together, I matter-of-factly told Nahum that I don't believe in dating. His jaw dropped to the floor and his face was full of shock and disappointment. As Therese began to explain what I meant, I simply told him that you can go out with Melissa only if your intent is to marry her. His face lit up with excitement and relief as it was obvious that his intent was proposal and marriage.

Over the next several months, Nahum and Melissa grew close and Nahum became part of our family. I know the Lord brought Nahum and Melissa together. In 1992, when I went on a missions trip to Romania (Chapter 4), we met up with Sean Larkin, a wonderful pastor from England and his seven-year-old son, Jonathan. By the end of the trip, we had bonded with both Sean and Jonathan and I promised Jonathan if he ever came to the U.S. that he could stay with us. Eighteen years later, Jonathan, who was now 25 years old, called me to see if I could help him connect to a church in the United States. I referred him to our church in San Diego, where he successfully landed a pastor's internship. Jonathan started leading a Bible study. It was at this Bible study that Nahum and Melissa met each other for the first time. There are no coincidences.

In December 2008, Nahum came to me and asked me if he could marry Melissa. I told him that I was honored and blessed that he came and asked me first … but it still didn't matter because the answer was absolutely not! I looked at him with a straight face and quickly told him I was just kidding. I knew they were both very happy and in love. I was also very excited that they were going to get married. Nahum and Melissa got engaged around Christmas time in 2008, and we started to plan for a wedding in 2009.

The first thing that Nahum and Melissa did was pray for the Lord to help them decide on a wedding date. They came to Therese and me and told us that they chose July 19th, the date our son Erin died as well as the date my wife's father died. Nahum and Melissa explained to us that July 19th was going to be a day of redemption. They hoped that the Lord would redeem that day as a day of life instead of a day of death, a day of new beginnings instead of endings, and a day of love, joy, and hope instead of a day of sorrow. They were hoping that the Lord would redeem Erin and Bill's death and use this day to remind us that life is more powerful than death.

Before I had told anyone that I was planning to write this book, I met to pray with a pastor friend of mine, Bruce. As I told him about the upcoming wedding and the redemption theme, he immediately asked me when I was going to write this book. I looked at him like a deer in the headlights–how did he know?–and then he told me that the title of the book would be Redemption. I was speechless.

When Nahum and Melissa told us their wedding day would be a day of redemption, I got chills. Then, when they told us they wanted to get married in our backyard, I went from chills to a cold sweat. How in the world were we going to get the backyard ready in time?

If you have ever been involved in the planning of a wedding, you understand just how much work is required. Wedding dress, bridesmaid dresses, invitations, colors, flowers, decorations, photography, vows, food, wine, wedding cake, etc. The list is endless and so is the cost! But, the planning for a wedding is fun! I love to plan for a vacation, a party, or a celebration. This was going to be all of these and much, much more. We were not just throwing a party, we were celebrating redemption! We were inviting our close friends and family to come and witness God's uniting of two young people for the rest of their lives. It was going to be a miraculous event.

And then it occurred to me, there is something else very exciting and joyful about preparing for a wedding. It is a reminder that we are called to prepare our minds and our hearts for Jesus just like a bride prepares for the bridegroom. We are to spare no expense, take no shortcuts, eliminate no details by examining our lives to be sure we are ready to meet Him.

> We are called to prepare our minds and hearts for Jesus just like a bride prepares for the bridegroom.

You see, in order to communicate His deep love for us, Jesus described His love in terms of a family. He compared Himself to a bridegroom who paid a steep price for his bride and then went to his father's house to prepare a place for her. A Hebrew bridegroom would work on his future home under his father's watchful eye. Not until his own father gave his approval that all was ready, could he go get his bride and bring her to see her new home. She wouldn't know when that time was coming; she simply had to be ready.

As we worked day and night getting the house ready–new driveway, roof, garage door, screens, house paint, new landscaping, repair and paint the fence, trim the trees, decorate the trees with lights and other decorations–that wedding analogy kept coming to mind and along with it the theme of redemption. As the groom paid the bride-price so he could have his bride, so Jesus paid the price so He could have a relationship with us. His redemption of us changes everything.

On the day of the wedding we were ready! Everything was set and the miracle unfolded before our eyes. The ceremony was amazing and we felt the presence of God. I will never forget walking down the aisle with my daughter–she was so happy! I looked into the eyes of my big and tough hunting buddy, Nathan, and he was crying and so that was the way it was … tears of joy!

At the reception we celebrated! My favorite part was when we played the Hebrew folk song "Hava Nagila." The title literally means "let us rejoice." It is clearly a song of celebration and is especially popular at Jewish weddings, festivals, and bar mitzvah events.

I had recruited several of the larger groomsmen to help with the raising of the bride and groom chairs. We put the two chairs out on the dance floor and sat the bride and groom down and then several groomsmen and other men picked them up and we all danced around them playing this outrageous Jewish folk song based on Psalm 118:24.

It was wonderful. Let us rejoice! For the bride and the groom are with us and we have been redeemed.

"But now a righteousness of God through the faith of Jesus Christ, toward all and upon all those who believe. For there is no difference, for all have sinned and come short of the glory of God, being justified freely by His grace through the redemption that is in Christ Jesus."

Romans 3: 22-24 (NKJV)

The Lord redeems His bride. He redeems our sorrows into joy! Let us Rejoice!

Douglas F. Wall

CHAPTER 23

HOLY FIRE!

"I'm going to be your grandpa! I have the biggest smile. I've been waiting to meet you for such a long, long while."

Billy Crystal

151

On the morning of March 15, 2012, our daughter Melissa texted us to let us know that she was in labor and was heading for the hospital. We arrived at Kaiser Anaheim hospital at around 9:30 a.m. and we found out that our granddaughter had just been born. Our baby had just given birth to a beautiful baby girl named Ember Grace. The miracle of experiencing the birth of seven children was eclipsed by the miracle of experiencing one of our children giving birth. I had no idea how God would reveal himself through the birth of Ember.

As I held Ember for the first time, I could feel the Holy Spirit as I bonded with her. It had been 16 years since we had a baby and I missed holding, kissing and loving a baby. Babies are special. Babies are innocent and they are completely dependent on others. One of the reasons babies are so wonderful is that they need us. They love to be loved. Through Ember, the Lord showed me how He feels about me and He wants me to be completely dependent on Him and need Him for everything.

If I would have known how awesome, wonderful and inspiring it was to have a grandchild, I would have skipped the parenting. Unfortunately, it doesn't work that way, but there is something simply amazing about being a grandfather that makes my pragmatic, serious personality fly out the window and my goofy, crazy, and fun personlity fly in. But Jesus said, *"Let the little children come to Me, and do not forbid them; for of such is the kingdom of heaven"* (Matthew 19:14, NKJV).

I do believe this is the Holy Spirit!

People were bringing little children to Jesus for him to place his hands on them, but the disciples rebuked them. When Jesus saw this, he was indignant. He said to them, "Let the little children come to me, and do not hinder them, for the kingdom of God belongs to such as these. Truly I tell you, anyone who will not receive the kingdom of God like a little child will never enter it." And he took the children in his arms, placed his hands on them and blessed them.

Mark 10:13-16 (NKJV)

The Lord redeems the lost child in each of us…innocence, dependence, and full of wonder.

Douglas F. Wall

REDEMPTION

EPILOGUE

During the last few years of my dad's life it was amazing to see his personality transform. After my mom passed away in 2005, my dad was very sad. He had lost his soul mate of 50 years and he became much more humble, patient and compassionate. He cried all the time. In the fall of 2008, my dad's health continued to decline and he slipped into a coma. I had the amazing experience as I held his hand for the last time and told him that if he ever gets into trouble to cry out to Jesus. He suddenly woke up, sat up and looked me in the eyes with clarity and purpose and said: "I love you son! I am proud of you!" ... and then he went back to sleep. He passed away a few hours later. I could not have asked for a better way to have my last talk with my dad.

I know that the Lord blessed me that day, waking him up from a death coma. I know this was a divine moment. I have often thought about why we are so sad when someone we are close to dies. We are sad because we miss them, we long to see them and talk to them again. We long to hug them, hold them and kiss them. Sometimes we regret that we did not get to properly say all the things we wanted to say. We often don't get a chance to forgive or ask for forgiveness.

God redeems it all. He redeems every mistake, every regret, every hurt, every failure, every loss, and every death. Jesus Christ is our redeemer and his grace, favor, redemption and power are infinite and available. My life is a testimony to that, and yours can be, too.

REDEMPTION

ABOUT THE AUTHOR

Douglas F. Wall is the Chief Executive Officer, Chairman and Co-founder of PureForge®, a technology company that makes metal tougher. PureForge® has initially focused on manufacturing brakes for life. Mr. Wall is a serial entrepreneur and experienced private equity investor, and has been an advisor to thousands of emerging growth companies.

Mr. Wall graduated from San Diego State University with a Bachelor of Science degree in Business Administration with an emphasis in Accounting. After graduating, he served as a senior accountant in the audit department of Arthur Andersen & Company and as a manager in the emerging business department of Ernst & Young before co-founding his first company, RCG Management. Mr. Wall serves as an advisor to several charitable organizations including: Good News to the Poor, The Charis Project, 2nd Mile Urban Ministries, Lavin Entrepreneurship Center at San Diego State University, and Point Loma University Entrepreneurship Program.

He is married to Therese, recently celebrated his 35th anniversary, and they have seven children—Melissa, Jessica, Courtney, Scott, Brent, Erin and Elise—and one grandchild, Ember. Mr. Wall is passionate about praying, inspiring, mentoring, participating in triathlons, hunting, fishing, writing, traveling, and spending time with family and friends. As an inspirational and motivational speaker, he lectures publically about his true stories of God's redeeming mercy and how they have impacted his life as well as the powerful lessons he has learned about the meaning and purpose of each and every life. Mr. Wall is also an author and philanthropist.

"I play the notes as they are written, but it is God who makes the music."

Johann Sebastian Bach

Soli Deo Gloria is a Latin term which means Glory to God alone.

It has been used by artists including Bach, Handel and Graupner to give glory and praise to God alone.